65 BUTTERCREAM FLOWERS

By RICHARD V. SNYDER

Decorating Cakes for Fun and Profit
27 Special Creations for Cake Decorators
28 More Floral Creations for Cake Decorators
29 New Floral Creations for Cake Decorators
65 Buttercream Flowers

65 Buttercream Flowers

by

RICHARD V. SNYDER

Owner and Director
The Snyder School of Cake Decoration
Detroit, Michigan

Illustrated

An Exposition–Banner Book

EXPOSITION PRESS NEW YORK

The basic buttercream recipes (Appendix E) are reprinted from *Decorating Cakes for Fun and Profit* (Exposition Press, 1953), pp. 121–23; copyright, 1953, by Richard V. Snyder.

First Edition, 1957
Second Edition, 1962
Third Edition, 1962
Fourth Edition, 1964
Fifth Edition, 1965

EXPOSITION PRESS INC., 386 Fourth Avenue, New York 16, N.Y.

*To all beautiful and wonderful flowers
everywhere, especially to my favorites:*

BESSIE E. SNYDER, my mother

CARLENE M. SNYDER, my wife

JEANNINE and DIANE, my daughters

Preface

THIS HANDBOOK, in reality the second volume of a "Decorating Cakes for Fun and Profit" series, can be used to good advantage by anyone who has learned the rudiments of cake-decorating. Readers of the first volume, *Decorating Cakes for Fun and Profit,* will be well prepared for the more advanced work described here. And we expect that even the most expert decorator can also profit from studying these flowers; the majority have never been published or even attempted before, and some of those that have been published elsewhere were not done with buttercream.

Frequent references are made throughout both to *Decorating Cakes for Fun and Profit* and to my other little book, *27 Special Creations for Cake Decorators.* However, when it was possible, repetition of actual material has been avoided to enable us to include more new and fresh subjects here. Instead, references to the two previous books are clearly marked, the abbreviation "DC" before a number indicating the page in *Decorating Cakes* and "27C" the page in *27 Special Creations.* (Note that in page references *f.* following a page number means "and the following page" and *ff.,* "and the following pages.")

Illustrations are numbered consecutively throughout the book (Figs. 1–85), and those with step-by-step demonstrations have the successive steps lettered *a, b, c,* etc., for easy reference.

7

(For instance, "Fig. 82*c*" refers to the third step in making calla lilies, as shown in illustration 82.)

It is hoped that the index will be useful. To make it so, references to both of my preceding books are included there when they seemed necessary. The appendixes listing flowers by color, by month, and by state adoption have been added to help the decorator co-ordinate his color-flower selection when planning a cake. The list of equipment and materials includes everything the decorator will need. If he has difficulty in securing anything mentioned in the text, he can obtain further information by mail from the Snyder School of Cake Decoration, 16841 Grand River Avenue, Detroit 27, Michigan.

Many of these flowers were tried out for the first time by small groups of graduate students before the text was written. These classes definitely helped us to find the best and clearest way of explaining certain techniques. Individual students have also contributed many excellent suggestions that are incorporated in this text for the benefit of all readers. It is impossible to give each student credit for his or her idea, but we wish to acknowledge our indebtedness and to express our gratitude generally to the graduate groups who were, as they expressed it, "guinea pigs for the book."

Grateful acknowledgement is also made to Mr. William C. Tucker, of the Grossman-Knowling Company, Detroit, who made the excellent photographs, and to Carlene M. Snyder, who, as a patient book widow, contributed ideas, objective criticism, and encouragement.

RICHARD V. SNYDER

Contents

65 BUTTERCREAM FLOWERS

FIGURE 1

CHAPTER I

Star and Star Pop-up Flowers

ANYONE who has used a star tube on a cake will be able to make the simple flowers in this chapter. Those who have never decorated cakes before will need to study and practice the work described in the first three chapters of *Decorating Cakes for Fun and Profit*,* the first volume in this series, before proceeding. But if you are an experienced decorator, you will find the star flowers easy and effective, and the star pop-up flowers novel and challenging.

BUTTERFLY BUSH

Make the butterfly bush (Fig. 1a) with several rows and layers of No. 27 lavender or dark-purple stars. Use three layers at the base, two layers in the middle, and one layer at the top. Use fewer stars in the second layer than in the first; use still fewer in the top layer. (This will make the bush look rounder.)

Add a No. 3 green stem to the base of each bush. Then, using a ⅛-inch V-cone (a paper leaf cone), add two or three leaves to each stem.

If you are not familiar with the paper-cone method of making leaves, study DC 41 ff.†

---

* Published by Exposition Press Inc. (1953, $4).

† Numbers preceded by the abbreviation "DC" refer to pages of *Decorating Cakes for Fun and Profit*. The abbreviation "27C" indicates pages of my *27 Special Creations for Cake Decorators* (Exposition, 1955, $1).

The term "⅛-inch paper V-cone" means that the widest part of the "V" opening is one-eighth of an inch across.

All models photographed in this book were made with buttercream decorating icing. Some of the flowers, including the star pop-up flowers on pp. 13 ff., have to be made with a formula very similar to the small and large recipes given on pp. 233 ff. Buttercream is easy to cut, and is very delicious. Another reason for its popularity as a decorating medium is that its soft texture resembles the texture of flower petals, so that flowers made of buttercream look very real.

Royal decorating icing (DC 124), stiff boiled icings, and other types of buttercream and fondant-buttercream icings can be used for many of the flowers. A large number of other food substances (DC 15) can also be used in decorating a large variety of food products.

A general list of equipment and materials used to make the flowers in this book is given in Appendix D (pp. 232 ff.).

LILAC

Make one layer of No. 27 lavender stars over the area to be covered (Fig. 1*b*). Make fewer stars in the second and third layers, so that the formation will be rounded on top.

Add a No. 4 green stem to the lilacs. Using a ⅜-inch V-cone, add leaves to the flower cluster. (Insert the V-cone under the edge of the lilacs before making some of the leaves.)

Lilacs may be made in pink, blue, lavender, or yellow.

When flowers occur in a variety of colors, the colors will be given in the instructions or text. No claim to completeness can be made, because present varieties are not fully catalogued, and new varieties are constantly being developed and discovered.

The Color Index of Flowers (Appendix A, pp. 225 ff.) should be very useful. When you have selected a specific color

14

scheme, you can turn to the alphabetical list of colors and find what flowers occur naturally in the colors you have chosen. (The Color Index includes all flowers demonstrated in this volume and all those in *Decorating Cakes for Fun and Profit*.)

HYACINTHS

Make a straight No. 3 green stem (Fig. 1c). Using a ⅛-inch V-cone and vertical leaf technique (pp. 45–47), form leaves of different lengths and curves (Fig. 1c).

Make one row of five No. 27 pink stars on the left side of the stem, starting the first one at the top and bringing the others downward (Fig. 1d). Make a similar row of stars to the right of the stem.

Then, placing the first star slightly higher than the other two on top, make a third row of five stars on top of the first two rows, down the middle (Fig. 1e).

Make a third leaf so that it overlaps the flowers slightly (Fig. 1f).

Hyacinths may be blue, white, red, yellow, pink, lavender, or purple. They are used on an Easter cake in *27 Special Creations for Cake Decorators* (p. 24). Other fantasy flowers are described in *Decorating Cakes for Fun and Profit* (pp. 27 ff., 38 ff.), and some are used in *27 Special Creations* (pp. 7, 10). Christmas trees are also made with star work in *27 Special Creations* (p. 22).

Blue thimble flowers and Veronica are other flowers that can be made with star work. You are urged to try your hand at making fantasy flowers of your own. Use star tubes, plain tubes, flower tubes, and plain paper cones. Thousands of imaginative flowers are waiting for you to create them.

SNOWBALLS

Using drop technique (DC 53 f.), make stems with a No. 3 brown cone (Fig. 2). Add tapered green leaves with a ⅜-inch

V-cone. (Study pp. 41 ff. to secure variety and naturalness in leaf arrangement.)

Make balls of white icing of different sizes with a No. 30 star cone and bulb technique (pp. 33 ff.), then cover them with stars. Make the snowballs irregular by adding a few extra stars on one or two sides. Make some high and oval, others medium high and round. Have some overlap others.

Add a few more leaves so that they overlap some of the flowers and some of the first leaves.

The snowballs in Figure 2 are made with a No. 30 star tube and white icing. However, you may also use pieces of cake covered with stars of white icing, or you may cover pieces of cake with boiled or fondant icing and roll them in short shredded cocoanut or angel-flake cocoanut.

Most of the flowers in this volume are arranged as they grow in nature. This gives you a truer understanding of your subject and makes it possible for you to portray flowers in their natural state.

Other arrangements should also be employed when they are appropriate: corsage, spray, wreath, basket, etc. You will find it helpful to study the chapter on flower arrangements (DC 57 ff.), the examples in Chapters VIII and IX in *Decorating Cakes for Fun and Profit,* and the illustrations in *27 Special Creations for Cake Decorators.*

As you learn to make a greater variety of flowers, use them in old arrangements—and the old arrangements will look new and fresh. (For other sources of new designs and new combinations of flowers, read DC 53.)

GOLDENROD

Drop a double-curved No. 3 green stem (Fig. 3). Make leaves with leaf-pressure technique (DC 29, 39 ff.) and a No. 3 cone, or make them with a ⅛-inch V-cone.

FIGURE 2

Using drawing technique (DC 27), add small No. 2 stems at irregular intervals to the large double-curved stem. (Make these small stems shorter as they approach the top of the arrangement.) With a very small paper-cone opening or a No. 1 tube, draw very short stems on the top side of some of the small stems. (Note two stems at lower left.)

Form flowers with a No. 13 star tube and golden-yellow icing. Pile two or three thickness of stars at the center of some arrangements to give more depth.

If you do not understand certain terms or techniques used here, check the index. You will be referred to pages in this book and in *Decorating Cakes for Fun and Profit* that will explain in detail what you need to know. We make liberal use of references throughout this text because we are trying to give help at the moment you may need it. (All references are to pages or illustrations in this volume unless the symbols "DC" or "27C" precede the reference.)

CANTERBURY BELLS

Before you begin making Canterbury bells (Fig. 4), check your No. 30 star tube carefully to be certain that all points are evenly opened and spaced. Be sure that the outside paper cone does not cover the lower half-inch of the metal tube.

Hold a No. 30 white cone in a vertical position and place the metal tube firmly against a cardboard surface. Exert pressure to form a flat star (DC 69 ff.; Fig. 4*a* below). Keep the metal tube firmly against the surface and continue pressure so that the star becomes larger and larger (Figs. 4 *b,c*), and finally pops up into a flower (Fig. 4*d*). Release pressure and lift tube out of flower.

Make seventeen or more of these "pop-up" flowers. Then add a small yellow center to each by inserting a No. 3 cone in the white icing, exerting pressure, and then gradually reducing pressure as the cone is brought upward (Figs. 4 *e,f*).

FIGURE 3

This is the cone star technique (DC 70 f.). If the flower tips sideways as it forms, tilt the cone in the same direction. (This will help to keep the flower from breaking apart.) The icing must be of medium consistency; if the flower does not pop-up, thicken the icing with a little sifted powdered sugar. If the flower pops up but also breaks apart, thin the icing with a few drops of water.

Next, drop No. 3 green main stems. Then draw short No. 2 stems at intervals along the main stems. Add some tapered, 3⁄8-inch V-cone leaves.

Remove the star pop-up flowers from the cardboard with a small knife and place them at the ends of the small stems. Tilt the Canterbury bells upward for the most part, and at various angles.

Using leaf-pressure technique and a No. 3 green cone, or a 1⁄8-inch V-cone, make several sepals (very small leaflike greenery) at the base of any flower where the base shows. Finally, add a few more tapered 3⁄8-inch V-cone leaves to the arrangement.

Canterbury bells are pink, lavender, purple, and white.

Other flowers can be made with the star pop-up technique; see morning-glories (pp. 22–23) and columbine (27C 9). Any size star tube may be used. Pop-ups made with a No. 13 resemble lilies of the valley.

One of the questions asked most often by readers of our previous books is, "Just what were the dimensions of the original models in the illustrations?" Except for the frontispiece (original model, 13½ by 16½ inches), most of them in this volume were done on 9-by-11-inch cardboards. Most of the photographic prints were 7½ by 8½ inches, which were reduced to their present sizes by the engraver. The largest illustrations in the book are about 4 by 5 inches. We hope that these specifications will help you visualize the original models more accurately.

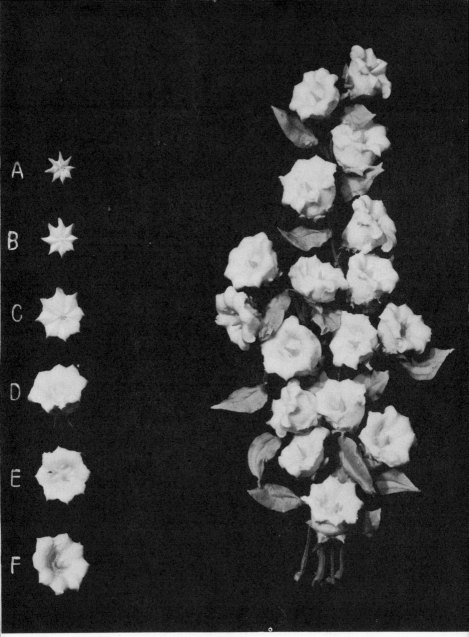

FIGURE 4

Tube sizes given in the text are those used in the models. They produced life-size flowers, in most cases. There were, however, exceptions—e.g., sunflower (pp. 78 ff.), dahlia (pp. 166–68), and others that were not apt to be produced full size on cakes.

Many times it is much better to use tubes smaller than those specified in the instructions. The size of the item being decorated and the kind of arrangement to be used often require miniature flowers.

MORNING-GLORIES

Using the same star pop-up technique that produced Canterbury bells (Fig. 4), make three No. 30 pink pop-up flowers (Figs. 5*a,b,c;* see frontispiece for full-color illustration of morning-glory, among other flowers).

Let the flowers dry for about fifteen minutes. Then, keeping the flower upright, hold the base of it between your index fingers and roll it back and forth until it is trumpet-shaped (Fig. 5*d*). Then pinch the top edges of the flowers and bend them downward slightly.

Shape others similarly. If the flowers are too sticky, let them dry longer or put some corn starch on your fingers.

Next, drop several winding No. 3 green stems so that some wind around each other. Add green buds (bulb technique, pp. 33 ff.) and tendrils. Make the bud at the left with No. 3 pink cone, and add sepals to it with a No. 3 green cone and leaf-pressure technique.

Make heart-shaped leaves with a ⅜-inch V-cone and a No. 3 green cone. (Study pp. 47–49 for this special leaf technique.)

Place trumpet-shaped morning-glories at ends of stems. Add sepals wherever they will show by using leaf-pressure technique and a No. 3 green cone. Finally, add several very small yellow dots to the center of each flower with a No. 2 cone.

Morning-glories are white, blue, purple, or red. They are

FIGURE 5

often striped. Striping can be done with a fine brush and vegetable color.

Some decorators use a simple syrup as a base for vegetable colors which they brush on icing or sugar work. Here is one recipe for simple syrup: Bring one pound of granulated sugar and one pint of water to a boil. Allow syrup to cool. Keep in a tightly-closed bottle when it is not in use.

Other bell-like and trumpetlike flowers can be made with the star-pop-up technique: cathedral bells, various kinds of columbine, foxglove, campanula. If you think of other possibilities for this technique (or for other techniques), please write us about them. We are also interested in any unusual arrangements or uses you find for the work that is described in our books.

FIGURE 6.

Chapter II

Gardenias and Inverted-Cone Flowers

GARDENIAS

THE METHOD for making a gardenia is a variation of the nail-rose technique. Regardless of your past experience in making nail roses (sometimes called full roses), you are urged to study *Decorating Cakes for Fun and Profit,* pp. 46 and 49 ff.; unless you understand the terms used there, the following explanations will be meaningless.

Put a little icing on a No. 7 flower nail. Press a 2-inch square of waxed paper against the icing and the nail disc. Using a No. 125 wedge-shaped flower tube in a paper cone of white icing against the waxed paper, make a cone of icing as for a rose (Fig. 6a).

Place the base of the tube at or near the *bottom* of this cone and make an open spiral (Fig. 6b). (Do not place the base of the tube at the *top* of the cone, as for a rose.) Using a 45-degree right tilt, make three petals that overlap very little or not at all, and are not higher than the spiral previously made (Fig. 6c).

For the last five or more petals, keep the tube at an extreme right tilt and hold the cone a little below the level of the flower-nail disc (Fig. 6d). Overlap some petals slightly, others not at all. Bring the base of the tube away from the center slightly as each petal is made, so that the upper surface of the petal is convex.

Using a little corn starch on the fingers to keep them from becoming sticky, touch the edges of the spiral and petals so that

25

FIGURE 7

they curl downward and look somewhat squarish. (This shaping can also be done after the flower has air-dried for fifteen or twenty minutes. In that case, it is not necessary to use corn starch.)

Place gardenia and waxed paper in the freezing compartment of a refrigerator for five minutes or more.

Drop a No. 3 stem of green. (See top arrangement in Fig. 6.)

With a No. 7 nail and a No. 125 white cone, repeat the work of Figures 6*a,b*. Keeping the tube in a straight position, make three overlapping petals, as for a rosebud. Trim bud with a knife, remove it from nail, and place it at the top of the stem.

Make sepals at the base of the bud with a No. 3 green cone and leaf-pressure technique. At a lower point on the stem make a large ball of icing with a No. 3 green cone. Now take the frozen gardenia out of the refrigerator and remove the waxed paper. Press gardenia firmly on the ball of green icing.

Insert a ½-inch V-cone of dark-green icing into the space under the flower. Gradually increasing the pressure as the cone is brought out from under the flower, make a ridged and rounded leaf (pp. 43 ff.). Gradually reduce pressure until the leaf comes to a point.

Form the rest of the leaves.

Make the gardenia corsage arrangement, shown at the lower right corner of Figure 6, in a similar way. (See also frontispiece.)

Another flower that can be made in much the same way is the camellia. The next flowers start out with a cone of icing in the center of a No. 7 nail. Outside of that, they have very little in common with nail roses, gardenias, or camellias.

HOLLYHOCKS

Make a No. 5 straight green stem. (See arrangement in Fig. 7.) Then, using bulb technique and a No. 3 green cone, make buds at top of stem, and large, rounded, irregular leaves with a ⅝-inch V-cone of green icing.

Using the method discussed in DC 49,* make a cone of icing on a No. 7 nail with a No. 125 white cone as though you were starting to make a rose (Fig. 7*a*). Holding the base of the tube at the *top* of the new cone, and tilting the tube to the right, make an inverted cone. As the inverted cone is being made, keep moving the top of the tube up and down to produce folds. Bring the last part of inverted cone under first part when finishing it (Fig. 7*b*).

Use a pair of scissors to remove inverted cone from top of original cone (Fig. 7*c*). Then use the flower nail to push the inverted cone off the scissors and to place it in the arrangement.

Using the original cone on top of the flower nail as a base, make more inverted cones and place them on the stem. (To make buds that are partly open, like the one near the top of the stem, tilt the tube only a trifle to the right when making an inverted cone.)

After the flowers are in the arrangement, insert a No. 3 cone of yellow icing into the base of each flower, exert pressure, and bring up a high center before stopping pressure (Fig. 7*d*).

This is a very simple and fast method of making these flowers. If you wish to take more time and to make a more nearly accurate reproduction of a hollyhock's five underlapped petals, use the method described on pp. 30 ff. for the Oriental poppy—which, however, has only four petals, and the center of which is radically different from that of the hollyhock.

Although we have tried to make the buttercream flowers in this and previous books as realistic as possible in appearance, we fully realize that they are not scientifically accurate. Scientific accuracy can be found in standard botanical books.

---

* "DC" indicates pages in *Decorating Cakes for Fun and Profit;* "27C," pages in *27 Special Creations for Cake Decorators.*

Our purpose is the artistic one of giving pleasure and inspiration by creating the essence of reality, an impression of reality, or the illusion of reality.

Hollyhocks are white, cream, yellow, pink, red, or maroon, single or double. When flowers occur in single and double form, we usually portray the single form, because that variety can be illustrated more clearly. Once the simple form is learned, it is not difficult to make a double variety.

Since hollyhocks are very tall, they can be used to good effect in the background of an arrangement or in front of a fence depicted in icing.

BLUEBELLS

With a No. 104 blue cone and a No. 7 nail, make a cone as for a nail rose (DC 49; Fig. 8*a* here).

The first three steps in making bluebells are the same ones used in making hollyhocks, pp. 27–29. Tilt tube to right and make a wavy inverted cone on top of the original cone (Fig. 8*b*). Remove inverted cone with a pair of scissors (Fig. 8*c*).

Drop a No. 3 green stem; and add some large, smooth, tapered leaves with a 1/4-inch V-cone. As the inverted cones are completed, place them in arrangement.

Use bulb technique (pp. 33 ff.) to add a cone of blue icing to the base of each inverted cone with a No. 3 tube (Fig. 8*d*). Smooth icing together with a moist brush.

With a very small paper-cone opening or a No. 2 tube, put several small yellow dots of icing in the center of each flower (Fig. 8*e*). Then add a bulb of green icing with a No. 2 cone to the base of each bluebell (Fig. 8*f*).

Wherever they will show, join bluebells to main stem with small No. 2 green stems.

Bluebells (sometimes called cowslips) are pink, blue, or lavender. Notice Appendix B, "Flowers of the Months," and

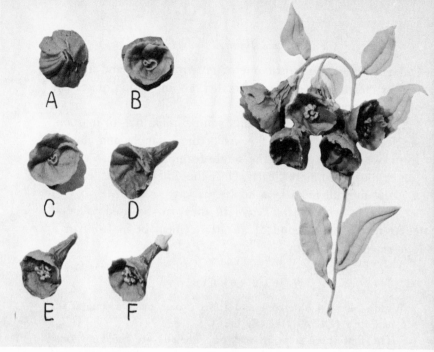

FIGURE 8

Appendix C, "State Flowers"; these lists may help you decide what flowers to use for a particular person or occasion.

ORIENTAL POPPIES

Form a cone as for a nail rose (DC 49), using a No. 125 red cone and a No. 7 flower nail (Fig. 9a). (Use nail rose outside petal technique [DC 50], that is, tilt No. 125 red cone to the right when making rest of poppy.) Turn nail halfway around and move tube up and down several times as you make first petal (Fig. 9b).

Starting the second petal halfway back of the first petal, turn nail halfway around and move tube up and down several times as the petal is formed (Fig. 9c). Form the third and fourth petals in the same way (Figs. 9d,e).

Trim base of flower with a knife as for nail roses (DC 50), and remove the flower from the nail with a knife and place it

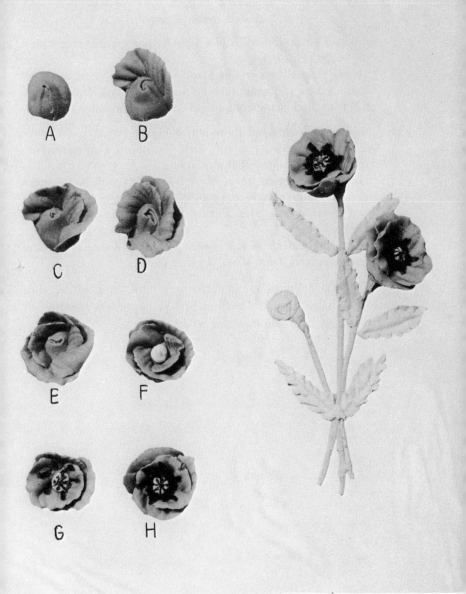

FIGURE 9

on a pan or cardboard. Add a light yellow-green center with a No. 5 tube (Fig. 9*f*.)

Using a small brush and black vegetable color, make small lines at center and wider lines on petals (Fig. 9*g*). Make a circle of No. 13 black stars around light yellow-green center (Fig. 9*h*).

Using the technique illustrated in Figures 18*c,d,* p. 50, make six or more leaves with a ¼-inch V-cone on a metal surface. Freeze them for three or four minutes.

Drop No. 3 green stems. Make bud at left with No. 3 green cone and bulb technique (pp. 33 ff.). Remove frozen leaves from metal surface with a sharp knife and place them in the arrangement.

Place poppies at ends of stems. Join each flower to its stem with some icing from a No. 3 green cone.

Oriental poppies are red, scarlet, pink, and white; they are especially popular with men. Many other varieties of poppies can be made in a similar fashion.

CHAPTER III

Bulb-Technique Flowers

A BULB-TECHNIQUE FLOWER with which you may be familiar
is the lily of the valley (DC 43 ff.).* Figure piping makes use
of this technique frequently—a clear example being the body
and head structure of a bird (DC 85).

When practicing bulb technique, use a small plain paper
cone with a small round opening at the end, or use a metal tube
with a plain round opening. The icing must be very soft.

Hold the cone at a 45-degree angle to the surface against which
you are working. Start with a light pressure. As soon as the
icing is fastened well to the surface, push the rim of the cone
or tube opening below the surface of the icing already placed,
and keep it below the surface.

Gradually increase pressure as you slowly lift tube *straight
up* from the surface against which you are working (but keep
the tube opening *below* the surface of the icing). When the ball
of icing is the size you wish, stop pressure and remove the tube
from the side of the ball.

If you wish to make a bulb of icing larger or higher, or if
you wish to change its shape in some other way, push tube opening into *side* of bulb, exert pressure on cone, and move tube in
appropriate direction. When the ball (or bulb) is the size and
shape you wish, stop pressure and remove the tube from the *side*
of the ball. (It is somewhat like pumping air into a bal-
loon.)

* "DC" indicates pages in *Decorating Cakes for Fun and Profit;*
"27C," pages in *27 Special Creations for Cake Decorators.*

In making the arrangement of snowberries in Figure 10, first drop several stems of No. 3 green icing. Using the suggestions on pp. 41 ff. for gaining variety in leaf structure and arrangement, add tapered leaves made with a 1/4-inch V-cone.

After practicing round bulbs of soft white icing with a No. 4 tube, add them to the arrangement in groups of different size and shape. Make some berries on top of others, and on most of them put a fine dot of black or dark-blue vegetable coloring with a pointed camel-hair brush or with a toothpick. Leave some of the berries plain so that we can imagine that the dots on them are hidden by the other berries in their groups.

Place additional leaves over some of the snowberries to obtain a more natural arrangement.

If you do not wish to have one of your more elaborate or favorite cake-top arrangements destroyed, study instructions on 27C 18; then you or the recipient of the cake can keep the arrangement for re-use later or as a souvenir. Many people refuse to cut into a beautifully decorated cake, or they cut into it very reluctantly. The solution offered on 27C 18 is also the best way out of that difficult dilemma.

BLEEDING HEARTS

Shaping each half of the flower like a carrot (Fig. 11*a*), keep the No. 3 cone opening below the surface of the initial bulb of soft pink icing and move the cone toward you in a curved line. As you start to finish the carrot-shaped bulb of icing, gradually release pressure and bring the cone down to the surface.

Make a second "carrot" to the right of the first one (Fig. 11*b*; notice that a crease is left in the center of the heart). Add two small pink petals at the base of the heart with a No. 2 cone (Fig. 11*c*).

FIGURE 10

Start a short No. 3 white line at, or slightly above, the base of the heart and bring it downward ¼-inch or less (Fig. 11*d*).

The leaf branch and the flower branch actually come out of a large vertical main stem at the right that is not shown. There are other invisible leaf branches and flower branches to the left and right of the invisible main stem. Notice that branches have flowers *or* leaves, but not both.

Using drop technique (DC 53 ff.), make branches with a No. 4 plain paper cone opening and brown icing. (The paper cone opening gives branches a slightly irregular surface: it makes them look more like wood.) Make very short stems for flowers, irregularly spaced on branch, with a No. 2 brown cone.

Make small light green leaves with a ⅜-inch V-cone. Form a large divided leaf at the end of each stem with three small leaves. Seal them together smoothly with moistened brush, knife, or finger. (Study pp. 43 ff. for special leaf technique.)

Add bleeding hearts of various sizes, shapes, and stages of maturity to ends of very short brown stems. (Notice that flowers at the lower left are not completely open and that the third flower from the right is turned sideways.)

Bleeding hearts are white or pink (see frontispiece). Other flowers that can be made with a similar technique are Dutchman's-breeches, red-hot pokers (torch lily), grape hyacinth, fuchsia, painted cup (Indian paintbrush).

Since there are many thousands of flowers and greenery, you may be more familiar with some varieties not illustrated here than with those we use. Some kinds of bleeding hearts, for example, have feathery green leaves instead of the kind shown in Figure 11.

It is best to use as models for the decorations on your cakes the varieties that grow or are available in your part of the country. Your neighbors will then recognize and enjoy your work even more.

FIGURE 11

FIGURE 12

FIGURE 13

HONEYSUCKLE

Drop a No. 2 green stem for the honeysuckle (Fig. 12). Using a ¼-inch V-cone, make light yellow-green leaves, tapered but not brought to a long, sharp point.

Form flowers and fruit with a No. 3 scarlet cone and bulb technique (pp. 33 ff.). Taper the fruit (notice the five at left of center).

Shape the ends of flowers (as in the case of the four at right of center) like lilies of the valley (DC 43 ff.). Intermix flowers and fruit in top cluster. Make flowers only in bottom cluster. Add two or three more leaves so that they overlap flowers.

AGERATUM

Drop green stems with a No. 3 cone (Fig. 13). Starting flowers just above stems, make an arc of No. 13 blue stars (Fig. 13a),

39

and fill in arc with more blue stars so that base of arc is level (Fig. 13*b*).

Form green base with No. 3 cone and bulb technique (Fig. 13*c*). Add second layer of blue No. 13 stars to arc to give illusion of depth (Fig. 13*d*). Make blue fuzzy tops with the very fine opening of a paper cone and the cone star technique (Fig. 13*e*; DC 70 ff.).

Make flower in center of arrangement with a round mound of No. 13 blue stars. (Notice small bud at lower right.)

Add heavily veined leaves with a ⅜-inch V-cone and method described on p. 44.

The ageratum is usually blue, but sometimes it is pale pink or white. You can make thistles, ironweed, and clover in much the same way.

We think you will enjoy practicing the great variety of leaves in the next chapter. It will help you make your arrangements more nearly accurate, natural, diversified, and interesting.

CHAPTER IV

Leaf Techniques

THIS CHAPTER contains many different ways of making leaves. Sometimes a particular leaf may be made by any one of several methods. Choose the method that is most effective for you under the conditions in which you work.

You are urged to study pp. 41 ff. of *Decorating Cakes for Fun and Profit,* which explain and illustrate the technique of making and using a paper V-cone. We use this type of cone for most leaves rather than the conventional metal leaf tube, for several reasons: It is more accurate and convenient, and we can make it the exact size we wish. We can change it from moment to moment to a larger and larger size just by snipping it a little more with a pair of scissors. At first we can make some fern or the very small sepals on flowers. When we snip it a little bit more, we can make some small leaves on stems. Then if we cut it more, we can make some medium-sized leaves. Finally we cut it still more and make large leaves. All of these can be made in the same arrangement in a very short time with a single paper V-cone. Before the cone is cut too large, it can even be cut straight across for making some stems. Then it can be cut V-style again for more leaves.

There are no metal tubes to clean after we finish. The paper cone is also the more versatile and is capable of producing more natural and beautiful work.

The angle of the V-opening can be cut to produce even or lopsided leaves. A sharp-pointed V-opening will produce a leaf that will not come to a point unless it is pointed afterward between thumb and finger. A 45-degree or blunter V-cone angle will produce a leaf that will point easily if the icing is soft and the pressure is reduced gradually before the final flick of the wrist. To some degree, the shape of the V-cone can even be changed so that it will fit the consistency of the icing.

Since paper is flexible, we can exert different pressures on the cone, and from different angles to the surface, to force the opening to close or to open wide, to close more on one side than on the other, to bend better on a curved leaf, or to produce many other subtle effects (which can be discovered only in practice).

Notice hand position, size of cone, and angle of cone to surface in Figure 14. The hand is cupped upward as the cone is brought away from the stem to which the leaf is joined. A gradual taper at the beginning of a leaf is produced by a gradual increase of pressure on the icing as the cone is brought away from the stem; and a gradual taper at the end of a leaf is produced by a gradual decrease of pressure on the icing. A final quick movement of the wrist that adds a sharp point to the leaf also tapers the icing just outside the cone, which is then ready for the beginning of the next leaf.

The cone is no longer than eight inches on each of its two equal sides before it is shaped; it can often be smaller, especially for ferns and small greenery. The cone is small enough and the icing is soft enough so that only the end of the thumb can apply the light pressure that is required. The angle between cone and surface (the angle beneath the cone) is 45 degrees, and the V of cone opening is almost horizontal to surface for flat leaf.

We shall refer to the leaves in Figure 14 as "horizontal leaves" because the V-cone opening starts most of them from that position. As you can see, however, many of these leaves do not finish with the V-cone opening in a horizontal position.

Practice the variations in leaf-making as a musician practices finger exercises in order to master all the shadings of tone of which his instrument is capable. In time, variations in leaf-making become almost automatic, and you will do the right thing easily and naturally.

HORIZONTAL LEAVES

Figure 14:

a) Form a smooth 45-degree leaf, tapered at both ends and pointed.

b) Tilt the horizontal V-cone opening to the right to a 45-degree diagonal. (The right side of the V-opening is higher than the left side.) Form a leaf similar to the first one.

c) Tilt the horizontal V-cone opening to left to a 45-degree diagonal. (The left side of the V-opening is higher than the right side.) Form a leaf similar to the first one.

d) Keeping the V-cone opening horizontal, use a low angle (20 degrees) between cone and surface and form a leaf similar to the first one.

e) Use a high angle (70 degrees) between cone and surface and form a leaf similar to the first one.

f) Form a leaf similar to first one but bring point downward.

g) Form a leaf similar to first one but bring point upward.

h) Form a leaf similar to first one but turn the last part of leaf to left.

i) Form a leaf similar to first one but turn last part of leaf to the right.

j) Form a twisted leaf by starting in horizontal position and gradually turning the V-cone opening almost upside down.

k) Start a leaf at the surface and form the rest of it off the surface.

l) Form a rounded leaf (used for trailing arbutus, p. 149)

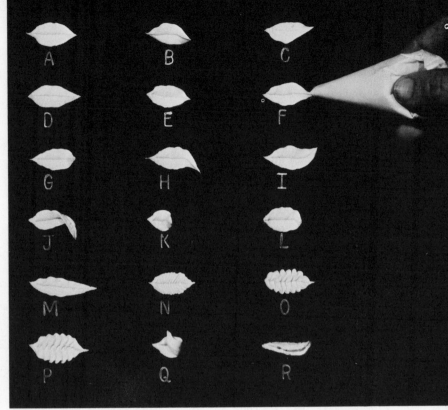

FIGURE 14

by reducing the pressure very little toward the end of the leaf, stopping pressure, and moving cone slowly to left or right before bringing cone away from leaf.

m) Form a long, narrow, tapered leaf.

n) Form a fine-veined leaf by moving tube back and forth only slightly.

o) Form a coarse-veined leaf by moving tube back and forth considerably.

p) Form a zigzag leaf by alternately moving the tube from left to right.

q) Touch up a leaf by hand after it is partially dry.

r) Bring up the leaf edges with the edge of a knife after the leaf is partially dry.

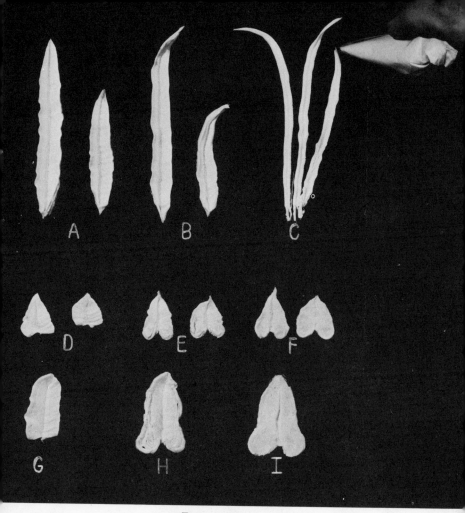

FIGURE 15

VERTICAL LEAVES

Hold a ⅜-inch V-cone opening in a vertical position; that is, the V-opening is on its edge (vertical) instead of being in a relatively horizontal position as before. (Notice hand and cone position in Fig. 15.)

Form a long wide straight leaf by keeping the same vertical position from the bottom to the top of the leaf (Fig. 15a).

FIGURE 16

Form a short wide leaf. (Do not change position of the wrist while leaf is being made.)

Form two more leaves similarly but twist the cone to the left as they are being finished (Fig. 15*b*).

Form three narrow vertical leaves similarly with a 1/4-inch V-cone (Fig. 15*c*).

Vertical leaves are used for all members of the daffodil family, pinks, tulips, lilies of the valley, some day lilies, cattails, and many others.

HEART AND CALLA LEAVES

Using a 3/8-inch V-cone and very soft green icing, make two leaves of different sizes (Fig. 15*d*; do *not* taper them at the base). Add enough of the same icing with a No. 3 cone to the base of both leaves to make them heart-shaped (Fig. 15*e*). Smooth the leaves with a moist finger or brush (Fig. 15*f*).

Then, using a 1/2-inch V-cone and a No. 3 cone, make a calla leaf in a similar way (Fig. 15*g*).

Add icing to the sides as well as the base of leaf (Fig. 15*h*); notice that calla leaf is a composite of bell and heart shapes. Smooth leaf with moist finger or brush (Fig. 15*i*).

Heart-shaped leaves are used for morning-glories, philodendron, and many others. The heart and calla leaves, and the divided leaves in Figure 16, can be made directly on the cake, or they can be made on metal and transferred to the cake after they have been frozen. As soon as they thaw, they can be shaped so that they do not lie too flat against the surface.

DIVIDED LEAVES

Using a 1/4-inch V-cone, make a long horizontal tapered leaf (Fig. 16*a*). Then make two small tapered leaves in V position near the base of the long one (Fig. 16*b*). Make two medium-sized tapered leaves in V position near the center of the large one (Fig. 16*c*). Smooth leaves together with water and brush, finger,

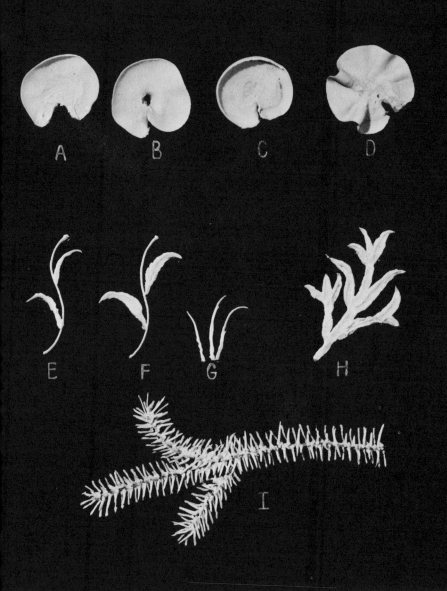

FIGURE 17

or knife, and put slight grooves in the leaf with the dull edge of knife (Fig. 16*d*).

Using a ¼-inch V-cone, put several leaves together, as in Figure 16*e*. Smooth them together. Add a No. 3 stem (Fig. 16*f*).

These leaves are known as "divided leaves." The one in Figure 16*d* is a chrysanthemum leaf. The one in Figure 16*f* is a complicated variety of peony leaf; a simpler kind is shown in the arrangement in Figure 66, p. 172.

Oak, maple, and grape leaves are especially attractive when made in this way.

FLOWER-TUBE LEAVES

Place against the surface of the cake the base of a No. 125 flower tube (a straight wedge-shaped tube) with green icing. Using the tube at a low angle (Fig. 36, p. 96) and a medium right tilt (Fig. 38*b*, p. 98), press icing with right hand and turn Lazy Susan or turntable with left hand to form water lily leaf (Fig. 17*a*); if it is not convenient to use a turntable of some kind, turn your right wrist and arm to the left; then, pressing the icing, turn your wrist and arm back to the extreme right. Make a complete round leaf by turning full circle (Fig. 17*b*). Fill in the hole left by base of tube with a No. 3 green cone and smooth the icing with moist brush or finger (Fig. 17*c*).

Form a nasturtium leaf (Fig. 17*d*) by moving the top of the tube up and down as the leaf is being formed, to give a wavy appearance. Fill in center hole with No. 3 green cone, and then make the icing smooth.

The heart-shaped type of violet leaf can also be made this way. After it is made, pinch the top part between finger and thumb to form a point.

FIGURE 18

You are urged to study DC 29, 39 ff.,* for plain tube leaf-pressure technique.

Using leaf-pressure technique and a No. 2 cone, make the simple leaves in Figure 17e by starting at the stem and pushing away from it. (Hold the end of the tube just off the surface.)

Make the simple leaves in Figure 17f with more pressure and a No. 3 cone. As pressure is increased to make leaf wider, lift the tube slightly, and as pressure is decreased, lower the tube to surface.

Make grasslike leaves with a No. 2 cone by starting at the base and pushing forward (Fig. 17g).

Make a complex monkshood leaf (Fig. 17h) by making several leaves with a No. 3 cone and then sealing them together with water and finger.

Make an evergreen twig with light-brown icing and a No. 3 cone (Fig. 17i). Then, using the very small opening of a very small paper cone of green icing, draw needles on both sides of the brown stems. (Slant needles toward the tip of the stem on which they grow.) Using cone star technique, make one row of needles at a 45-degree right diagonal up from the stem, and then a similar row of 45-degree-angle left diagonal needles. (Fasten each needle to its brown stem and pull up to a point. Do not overextend the needles, or they will curl and spoil the effect.) Using the same cone star technique, bring one row of needles straight up from the centers of the stems.

A little powdered sugar sifted over the twig will make it look as though it were covered with snow. The evergreen twig

---

* "DC" indicates pages in *Decorating Cakes for Fun and Profit;* "27C," pages in *27 Special Creations for Cake Decorators.*

can be put to good use on Christmas holiday cakes and on cakes for men.

Use cone star technique, small cone openings, and green, brownish green, or brown icing to produce thorns on rose stems and others. Notice the thorns on the 3-D rose, Figure 50, p. 129.

ROUGH-EDGED LEAVES

Using a ¼-inch V-cone opening in a horizontal position and a steady continuous pressure on the icing, bring the cone from the starting point at the base to a point just a short distance from it and stop (Fig. 18*a*). Then move the cone another short distance from the base and stop. Vary both the distances and the time intervals between a series of stops, but keep a steady, continuous pressure on the icing until pressure is reduced at the last for a tapered leaf. (This is called "back-away technique.")

If you wish a smoother surface on the leaf, press it gently with moist brush or finger. (Fig. 18*b*).

Form tapered horizontal leaves with a ¼-inch V-cone on a metal surface (Fig. 18*c*). Freeze them and then cut the edges in irregular fashion with a paring knife to produce a poppy-type leaf (Fig. 18*d*).

Freeze them a second time. Then remove them from metal surface with a sharp knife and place them in flower arrangement. As they thaw, bend the leaves to any desired shape.

Make curved tapered leaves for holly (Fig. 18*e*) directly on the cake or on a metal surface with a ⅜-inch V-cone and very soft icing. Using a small brush and water, make curved lines from center of leaf to edge. Push the brush down slightly toward the end of each curved line to form a point beyond the edge of the leaf (Fig. 18*f*).

Using a No. 3 red cone and bulb technique (pp. 33 ff.), make holly berries on leaves and in between them.

Daisy leaves, oak leaves, and others of the same type can be produced quickly with the back-away technique used in Figures 18*a,b*.

FILL-IN LEAVES

Draw or trace the outline of an ivy leaf on a sheet of paper (Fig. 19*a*). Place the paper on top of a cake, and using the lines as a guide, punch holes through the paper and into the cake top with a pin.

Remove the paper and drop a No. 3 green line on the pin-holes in the icing (Fig. 19*a*). Fill in ivy-leaf outline with a No. 5 cone of *soft* green icing (Fig. 19*b*). Smooth icing with water and brush or knife (Fig. 19*c*).

If you are skillful at drawing, you may dispense with the intermediate steps and draw or drop the outline of icing directly on the cake top. You can also make the leaves on a metal surface, freeze them, remove them with a sharp knife, arrange them on the cake, and shape them as you wish when they start to thaw.

The fill-in method may be used for other leaves, for flat flowers, for cartoons and other pictures (27C 5, 14, 15).

FREEZE-AND-SHAPE LEAVES

Using a ⅜-inch V-cone, form a short, ridged, horizontal leaf and a long smooth leaf on a metal surface (Fig. 19*d*). Put them in the freezing compartment of a refrigerator for three or four minutes.

Form mounds of green icing where you intend to place the leaves (Fig. 19*e*). Remove frozen leaves from metal surface with a sharp knife and place the base of each leaf against the cake and center on top of mound of icing (Fig. 19*f*).

When the leaves start to thaw, bend their edges downward to give them a different contour and to hide mounds of icing that are supporting them (Fig. 19*g*).

Make a variety of three leaves with a ⅜-inch V-cone against a metal surface and freeze them (Fig 19*b*). Remove frozen leaves from metal surface with a sharp knife. As they start to thaw, curve them over a rounded cardboard surface, or curve them and place them on edge on a flat cardboard surface (Fig. 19*i*). Allow them to dry overnight. (The cardboard acts like blotting paper and speeds the drying.)

Put base of dried leaves in fresh icing and stand them upright in an arrangement (Fig. 19*j*).

We do not recommend that all leaves in an arrangement should be the frozen-and-shaped variety. To make them would be very time-consuming. We do suggest that you use a few now and then among your other leaves to add variety and a three-dimensional quality to your work.

The dried leaves can be stored for weeks in a closed container and for an indefinite time in a freezing cabinet.

COLORING LEAVES

The methods described for the coloring of leaves may also be applied to the coloring of stems, flowers, borders, writing, and figure piping. Use the method for filling cones and for variegating the colors in cones described in DC 21 ff. Remember to increase the thickness of the icing layer toward the top of the cone.

Place light green icing on opposite sides of the cone (Fig. 20*a*). Fill the center of the cone with darker green icing pressed from a second cone. Cut the V-cone opening so that dark icing is at the point and light icing is on either side when the leaf is formed.

Place dark green icing on opposite sides of cone (Fig. 20*b*); fill center of cone with lighter green icing pressed from a second cone, and cut the V-cone so that light icing is at the point and the dark icing on either side when a leaf is formed.

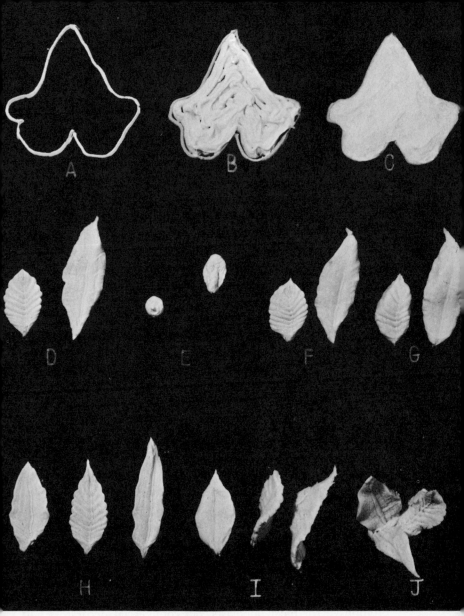

FIGURE 19

Using the same method, make a leaf with a green center and brown edges (Fig. 20*c*).

Put a little brown along one side of cone (Fig. 20*d*). Fill the rest of the cone with green icing and cut the V-cone so that brown icing comes out of right side of V-opening when leaf is formed.

Fill one side of a cone with light green icing (Fig. 20*e*); fill the other side with dark green icing. Cut the V-cone so that top of leaf is dark green and underside is light green. Twist the leaf as it is being formed in order to show contrast.

Put several different amounts of brown and green alternately in a cone (Fig. 20*f*) and make mottled brown and green leaf.

Form green leaf (Fig. 20*g*) and brush the edges of it with brown vegetable color. (See below about the use of an air brush.)

Form green leaf (Fig. 20*h*) and add brown icing with a No. 2 cone around the edge and put several dots in the center of the green leaf. Smooth leaf with water and brush, knife, or finger.

Form drops of dew on rose and leaves with a very small cone of clear piping jelly and bulb technique (Fig. 20*i*). Or brush buttercup and leaves with lukewarm, clear piping jelly for unusual shiny and glistening effect (Fig. 20*j*).

Many interesting effects can be achieved with a brush and warm piping jelly—for example, it gives the petals of begonias their natural waxy appearance. Piping jelly can be purchased from bakery-supply houses and mail-order houses.

Commercial airbrushes are used for coloring leaves, flowers, and other decorations and for whole cakes, for they produce beautiful and unusual effects that can not be duplicated as effectively or quickly in any other way. The use of stencils with airbrush equipment is also gaining in popularity. The cost of the equipment—about fifty dollars, more or less—makes it prohibitive for most hobbyists, but commercial decorators will find it practical. If you are interested, contact a commercial artists'-supply house or a bakers'-supply house.

FIGURE 20

FIGURE 21

We do not recommend the use of inexpensive equipment into which the decorator forces his breath. The use of such apparatus for the coloring of food is definitely unsanitary.

LEAF ARRANGEMENTS

The way in which leaves are placed in relation to the flowers has a great deal to do with the beauty and the naturalness of the arrangement. Figures 21*a–d* each have two flowers in approximately the same relationship to each other, and each grouping has approximately the same number and size of leaves. Notice, however, how different the arrangements are because the leaves are placed differently.

Using a ⅜-inch V-cone, form the leaves first. Then place two apple blossoms (pp. 136–45) on top of them. (Fig. 21*a*. Notice that this method tilts flowers at different angles.)

Place two apple blossoms on a flat surface. Using the same leaf cone, start leaves under the edges of the flowers as far as possible and bring them away from the flowers. (Fig. 21*b*. Notice the open look. The flowers are flat, but the leaves show more completely.)

Place two apple blossoms on a flat surface. Using the same leaf cone, start leaves under the flowers and bring them above or over flowers. (Fig. 21*c*. Notice that this method adds a certain naturalness.)

Form two leaves first. Place two apple blossoms against the leaves. Then start two leaves from under the edges of the petals and bring them away from flowers. Start the last two leaves from under the edges of the petals and bring them above or over the flowers. (Fig. 21*d*. Notice that we combined the three methods in one arrangement, because all three have their good points.)

We suggest that you turn to the large apple-blossom arrangement in Figure 54 (p. 142) and study the application of the methods you have just learned. These methods can be used to good advantage with many flowers: snowballs (Fig. 2), Canterbury bells (Fig. 4), snowberries (Fig. 10), honeysuckle (Fig. 12), calla lilies (Fig. 80), and others.

STEM AND LEAF CONTRAST

Make one large stem with a No. 3 green cone (Fig. 21e). Then make two small stems coming out from the large one.

Using a ⅜-inch V-cone, add leaves so that two of them overlap stems.

Notice that this leaf and stem overlapping adds interest, naturalness, and depth to an arrangement. The stems can also overlap the leaves.

Make similar stems with the same No. 3 green cone (Fig. 21f). Touch up stems with brush and brown color; add leaves as before.

Notice the greater contrast between leaves and stems. The stems could have been made a darker or lighter green than the leaves, or the stems could have been made with a combination of green and brown icing, or with just brown icing.

Make similar stems with the same No. 3 green cone (Fig. 21g). Add leaves as before and touch up edges of leaves with brush and brown color, especially where they overlap stems.

Notice that this helps to separate leaves and stems. The contrast could also have been secured by making leaves a darker green, by using a combination of green and brown icing, or by brushing the edges of the leaves with a darker green.

Make similar stems with the same No. 3 green cone (Fig. 21h). Brush stems with some brown color, and make some leaves overlap each other. Touch edges of leaves with brush and brown color, especially where they overlap.

Notice that the brown color separates the leaves from each other and makes them more attractive. The separation could also have been achieved in the other ways described above.

You will also enjoy the variety of so-called greenery in the next chapter. Some of it is not really green; nevertheless, we think that you will find it attractive and useful.

FIGURE 22

CHAPTER V

Other Greenery

PUSSY WILLOWS

Make three wavy No. 3 brown stems (Fig 22*a*). Add three green buds with No. 3 cone to the lower part of stem at left. (Notice that where the stem bends to the right the bud forms to the left, and vice versa.)

Make the three pussy willows above the buds with a No. 4 cone of light yellow-green icing and bulb technique (pp. 33 ff. Notice that those in this intermediate stage look something like boxing gloves.)

Make the two pussy willows at the top of the stem with a No. 3 white cone and bulb technique. Add light-gray color with brush to lower part of each white bulb.

Make mature pussy willows on the other two stems as you made the two at the top of the left stem, and add brown sepal-like bases to most pussy willows on all three stems with a No. 3 brown cone. (Some sepal-like bases are hidden.)

CATTAILS

Using a ⅛-inch V-cone of light green icing, make several vertical leaves (pp. 45–47) with various curves (Fig. 22*b*). Using a still lighter shade of green icing, make a few more vertical leaves. Then drop three No. 3 green stems that are almost straight.

Hold a No. 4 cone of soft reddish-brown icing in a horizontal position and form cattails with bulb technique. Then add a small spike of green icing to the top of each cattail.

Form several more light green and very light green vertical leaves in front of stems and other leaves.

Notice that the use of two different shades of leaves gives the illusion that the lighter underside of some leaves is showing or that the sunlight is being reflected more by some leaves than by others.

Drop stems with a No. 3 brown cone (Fig. 22c. A paper-cone opening makes the stems look like wood.) Add very small stems for berries and leaves with a fine paper-cone opening and brown icing.

Using a No. 2 orange cone and bulb technique, make bittersweet berries in upper left part of arrangement. (Bring berries to fine point at top.) Then, using a ⅛-inch V-cone of orange icing, form three leaflike parts for each berry that has burst open. With a No. 2 scarlet cone and bulb technique, form a round scarlet seed at the center of each orange shell that has broken.

Using a ⅜-inch V-cone of green icing, form tapered leaves at ends of small stems. Make an extra long point on each leaf by pinching the icing between finger and thumb when it is almost dry. Rough the edges of the leaves with a sharp knife or a razor blade. (See frontispiece.)

MISTLETOE

Drop No. 3 stems of medium green icing (Fig. 22d). Using a No. 2 cone of cream-white icing and bulb technique, form round mistletoe berries. Add a dot of brown color to most of them with a toothpick or fine brush. (Snowberries in Fig. 10, p. 35, are larger but similar.)

Make a 3/16-inch V-cone so that the leaves will be gray green on top and yellow green on the underside. (See Figure 20e and pp. 54–58 for coloring method.) Form leaves of various sizes; angle some and twist others (Fig. 14j, p. 44) so that the light-colored underside of some leaves is visible.

Give each leaf a long, narrow taper at the beginning (Fig. 14m, p. 44) and a large, wide roundness at the end (Fig. 14o).

If you would like to make shamrocks, study DC 83 ff.*
Four-leaf clovers can be made similarly. They can be used for
a "Happy New Year" cake or to wish someone good luck, or
as a 4-H Club emblem.

PINE TREE

Make the trunk of a pine tree with a No. 5 cone of brown icing,
with bulb technique (Fig. 23*a*). Make branches of different
lengths with horizontal leaf technique (pp. 43 f.) and a 3/16-inch
V-cone. Bring some branches toward you for a three-dimensional
effect.

MAPLE TREE

Make the trunk of a maple tree with a No. 5 cone of brown
icing, with bulb technique (Fig. 23*b*). Using very soft green
icing and a No. 5 plain paper cone, make foliage thick in center
and thin at edges.

Stir icing around and in various directions with a brush.

PAINTING WITH ICING

Use some white icing on all sides of the pine tree, and here and
there on the tree branches; stir it around with a brush. The result
will look like a snow scene in the north woods. Use some light
green and some dark green icing on either side of the pine tree
to give the illusion of near-by shrubbery and distant forests.

Use some smooth sky-blue icing as a background. Add the
maple tree or any other kind. Use some green icing in the foreground to represent grass, and white icing with a touch of gray
here and there to represent clouds in the distance.

Painting with very soft icing is easy and very effective,

---

* "DC" indicates pages in *Decorating Cakes for Fun and Profit;*
"27C," pages in *27 Special Creations for Cake Decorators.*

especially when it is used to create background in this way. It can be used on the sides of cakes as well as on the tops.

When you are making buttercream icing very soft, thin it with egg white instead of water; then the shortening and sugar will not separate.

You can also paint scenes on icing with liquid vegetable colors or with colors that have been mixed first with simple syrup or with lukewarm piping jelly (pp. 54–58). A combination of colored-icing work and liquid-color work can produce practically any effect, depending upon one's skill with a brush. You can also successfully combine tube and brush work. (Notice brush work, 27C 4, 15, 16, 17.)

CACTUS

Holding a No. 30 yellow-green cone horizontal to the surface, start pressure at the base and gradually reduce pressure as you bring tube to the top of the cactus.

Place a No. 27 cone of the same icing beneath the surface of the trunk, exert pressure, and bring small branches to the left, right, and directly toward you. Make smaller branches come out of some of the small branches.

Make the barrel-like cactus with a No. 30 star cone held in a horizontal position. (Pressure is constant.) Add pink dots to the top to represent flowers.

Make cactus at right with a No. 3 cone of soft green icing and bulb technique, shaping it like a bunch of watermelon seeds stuck together. Add needles with a very fine paper-cone opening.

PALM TREE

Make trunk of palm tree (Fig. 23c) with a No. 5 cone of light yellow-green icing. (Make the base larger than the rest of the trunk.)

Using a ⅜-inch V-cone of medium green icing, make several tapered leaves on a metal surface; freeze them; remove them

Figure 23

FIGURE 24

with a sharp knife, shape them, and let them dry on cardboard for several hours or overnight. (See pp. 53 f. for technique.)

Make several leaves directly on cake. Then add several of the dried leaves so that they stand out from the surface, and brace them underneath with some green icing.

Using a No. 2 cone of green icing, make diagonal lines on each leaf as in the method for making fern (pp. 69 f.). Make a line down the center of each branch to cover loose ends of the diagonal lines.

Figure 23 gives us greenery that can be used to indicate foliage of most sections of the earth that have it. This can be useful for *bon voyage* cakes and for good-luck cakes for friends who move to different parts of the country or the world.

RATTLESNAKE FERN

Make a very small paper cone that has been brought to a sharp point; fill it with about two teaspoons of soft dark-green icing, and close the top carefully. Cut the cone opening so that it is about No. 1 in size.

Drop a long curved stem (Fig. 24a). Draw left and right matching small stems that almost start at the same place on the main stem and curve upward. (Make small stems shorter as they near the top of the main stem.)

Using a very small 3/32-inch V-cone of soft light green icing, add leaves to the small stems. (Fig. 24b.)

(Notice that leaves become larger from the point of small stem toward main stem. All leaves on longer stems are larger. Leaves are angled upward toward the end of each small stem, and are at different tilts and angles, with some overlapping.)

INTERRUPTED FERN

Using a stem cone as described above, make long and small stems straight (Fig. 24c). Then make some short stems just above longer stems at base. (Hence its name, interrupted fern.)

Holding a No. 2 cone of soft light-green icing straight down and using leaf-pressure technique (DC 29, 39 ff.), make rounded leaves, arranged as for rattlesnake fern (p. 69). Touch leaves lightly with moistened finger after they are made in order to make them thinner.

MAIDENHAIR FERN

Drop main stems with a No. 2 reddish brown cone (Fig. 24*d*) and draw small stems with No. 1 reddish-brown cone so that they slant slightly toward end of main stem.

Using a No. 1 round cone opening and soft green icing, make three or four short downstrokes for each leaf (Fig. 24*e*.) Touch the top part of each leaf with a moist finger to make it smooth. (Be careful to retain points at the lower edge of the leaf.)

MUSHROOMS

Using bulb technique (pp. 33 ff.) and figure-piping method of making brim of witch's hat (DC 86), form mushrooms of different sizes and at different angles with a No. 3 cone of soft cream-white icing (Fig. 24*f*). Using icing or a brush and vegetable color, show brown on the underside when a mushroom is tilted appropriately. (Mushrooms are often found near fern and can be used in a scene with them.)

PHILODENDRON

Drop a No. 3 green stem in a zigzag pattern. (Fig. 24*g*). Draw No. 2 short green stems which branch off to left when main stem turns to right, and vice versa.

Using a No. 2 brown cone, make a leaflike bit of husk at the point where each small stem leaves the main stem. Using a 1/4-inch V-cone of green icing, make heart-shaped leaves on short stems. (See Figure 15*f*, p. 45, for special leaf technique.) Make a very long point on each leaf by pinching the icing between thumb and finger after the leaf is made. (Notice that main stem goes beyond the small stem of last leaf to the right.)

Drop a straight No. 3 green stem (Fig. 24*b*). Then make scarlet leaves with a ⅛-inch V-cone at the top. Cut the same cone larger and make the rest of the leaves with a ¼-inch V opening.

Add green edges to leaves, or use a scarlet-and-green variegated cone in the first place. Use cream-colored icing in the center of each leaf. (See pp. 54–58 for special color techniques.)

Smooth leaves with moist brush or finger. Make veins in leaves with a knife edge. (Dip knife in water if it sticks to the icing.)

Coleus leaves are colored fantastically: bronze, pink, apricot, cream, green, etc. Coleus, philodendron, or fern can be used as the main decoration on a cake. They are attractive enough in themselves. (Notice the use of ferns and other greenery in the frontispiece.)

Flowers are also made with various leaf techniques. There are many interesting examples in the next two chapters.

FIGURE 25

CHAPTER VI

Leaf-Technique Flowers

FORSYTHIA

TWO METHODS are given for forsythia: metal-surface and direct. (See frontispiece.) Metal-surface technique is described at greater length in Chapters IX and XIV:

Make four tapered leaves against a metal surface with a 3/16-inch V-cone of pale-yellow icing (Fig. 25a–d), press the centers smooth with a moist finger, and add a small dot of yellow icing.

Place the metal surface in the freezing compartment of a refrigerator for three or four minutes. Then take it from refrigerator and remove the flower with a sharp knife. Place the flower on a small ball of yellow icing (Fig. 25e) and bend the petals in any shape you wish as soon as they start to thaw.

In the direct method, which is faster, make a small ball of yellow icing with a No. 3 cone directly on the cake (Fig. 25f). Begin each of four leaflike petals at the top center of the ball of icing, bringing the ends of some petals away from surface when finishing them (Fig. 25g–j). Touch the center of the flower with a moist finger to make it smoother, and place a No. 3 yellow dot of icing in center of flower.

Drop No. 4 brown stems a little straighter than usual; then add short No. 2 green stems to large brown stems. Add little balls of green icing to some of the short green stems to indicate flower buds.

Using the direct method, make flowers of various sizes at different angles, and at various stages of development.

FIGURE 26

The direct method of making forsythia was used in the arrangement shown in Figure 25. If the metal-surface method is used instead, make several rows of flowers on a metal surface and freeze them for a few minutes. Then put balls of yellow icing at ends of small stems. Take the flowers out of the freezer, loosen them from the metal surface with a sharp knife, and place them on the balls of icing. As soon as the petals thaw enough to become flexible, shape them in various ways to give the arrangement a natural appearance.

Forsythia are pale yellow, bright yellow, or gold.

Another leaf-technique flower that is used a great deal during the Christmas holidays is poinsettia (DC 43),* which is used in a wreath with holly in 27C 22. Some other interesting flowers to try are trillium, adder's-tongue, and scarlet sage.

CROCUS

Holding a white ¼-inch V-cone opening in a horizontal position, bring a long tapered petal toward you (Fig. 26*a*). Tilting the V-cone opening to a right diagonal position, make the second petal on the right edge of the first one (Fig. 26*b*). Tilting the V-cone opening to a left diagonal position, make the third petal on the left edge of the first (Fig. 26*c*).

Then, holding the V-cone opening in a horizontal position, make a fourth petal down the center (Fig. 26*d*). Tilting the V-cone opening to left diagonal position, overlap the right edge of the fourth petal with petal number five (Fig. 26*e*). Finally, tilting V-cone opening to right diagonal position, overlap the left edge of the fourth petal with petal number six (Fig. 26*f*).

Using a No. 3 white cone in a horizontal position and bulb technique (pp. 33 ff.), lengthen and taper the base of the crocus (Fig. 26*g*). Smooth the spot where leaf and bulb work join with a moist brush or finger. (Figure 26*h* shows the flower right side up.)

Make each crocus independent of the others. (Notice that an unopened crocus is tapered at the top. The one in Figure 26*h* is an example.) Partly open some of the flowers in the arrangement by bringing a few of the petals away from the center as they are being finished.

---

* "DC" indicates pages in *Decorating Cakes for Fun and Profit;* "27C," pages in *27 Special Creations for Cake Decorators.*

Make some flowers smaller in order to give perspective to the arrangement. Make just small white marks for those that are farthest away.

Use leaf pressure technique and a No. 3 green cone to make grasslike leaves at front, back, and sides of flowers.

This arrangement against a cake iced in very light green is excellent decoration in early spring. The light-green icing can be combed in various directions to represent grass. Use a variety of colors for the flowers. Crocuses also make a beautiful border at the base of a cake.

The crocus can be made in white, yellow, lavender, purple, striped lavender and white, striped blue and white. Variegate colors in a leaf cone for the striped varieties. (See pp. 54–59 for leaf-coloring technique.)

For a different effect, make flowers on a metal surface, freeze them, air-dry them on cardboard overnight, and place them on top of the cake in an upright position.

SNOWDROPS

Using a 1/4-inch V-cone of white icing at a 45-degree angle, make a tapered mound of icing by gradually increasing pressure and lifting cone, then gradually decreasing pressure and lowering cone (Fig. 27a).

Using leaf technique, tilt the V-cone opening to a right diagonal position and make a tapered petal on the left side of the tapered mound of icing, moving from the top to the bottom (Fig. 27b). Then, holding the V-cone opening in a horizontal position, make the second tapered petal over the center of the mound (Fig. 27c). Tilt the V-cone opening to a left diagonal position and make a third tapered petal over the right side of the mound (Fig. 27d). The rest of the petals are not shown.

Brush the ends of three petals with green vegetable color (Fig. 27e). Make small ball of icing at top of snowdrop with a No. 3 green cone (Fig. 27f).

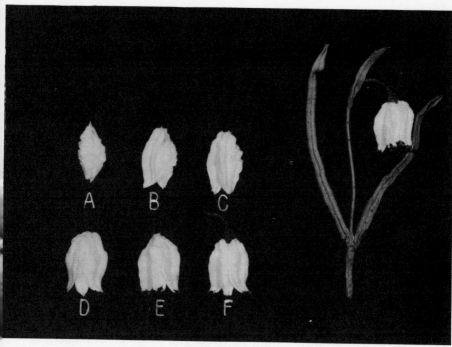

FIGURE 27

Drop a stem in the shape of a candy cane with a No. 3 green cone.

Using a 3/16-inch V-cone of green icing, start both of the large leaves at the bottom of the stem. Bring them upward along the stem an inch or so, and then bring them away from the stem. (Use vertical leaf technique described on pp. 45–47.) Make a small leaf where the stem bends to the right.

Form the snowdrop slightly below the end of the stem. Join the flower to the stem with a small ball of green icing.

GENTIANS

Holding a blue 3/16-inch V-cone opening in a horizontal position, bring a long tapered petal toward you (Fig. 28a). Tilting the V-cone opening to a right diagonal position, make the second petal on the right edge of the first one (Fig. 28b), and tilting

V-cone opening to a left diagonal position, make the third petal on the left edge of the first one (Fig. 28c).

Tilting V-cone opening to a left diagonal position, fasten the fourth petal to the right edge of the second petal (Fig. 28d). Tilting V-cone opening to a right diagonal position, fasten the fifth petal to left edge of third petal and to the left edge of fourth petal (Fig. 28e).

Using bulb technique (pp. 33 ff.) and a No. 3 blue cone in a horizontal position, lengthen and taper the base of the gentian (Fig. 28f). With a moist brush or finger, smooth the place where bulb and leaf work join. Make No. 3 green sepals at base of flower with leaf pressure technique (Fig. 28g. Figure 28h shows the flower right side up.)

Drop No. 3 green stems. (Notice that short stems branch out from long one.)

Using a 3/16-inch V-cone, make small tapered leaves by twos. Twist and curl some of them (pp. 43 f.). Make a bud at the extreme right with a No. 3 blue cone and bulb technique.

Start gentians 1/4-inch above the tops of stems. Join flowers to stems by lengthening the flowers with a No. 3 blue cone. Make green sepals at base of each flower.

SUNFLOWERS

Drop a straight stem with a No. 5 green cone (Fig. 29), and add short No. 3 green stems for the leaves and a longer one for the bud.

Make the bud with a No. 3 green cone and bulb technique. Cover the ball with little green cones of icing made with No. 3 tube and cone star technique.

Using a 3/8-inch V-cone, tilt and twist (pp. 43 f.) large, tapered leaves as you join them to the short leaf stems.

Make the sunflower at the top of the large stem.

With a pin draw a circle 1½ inches in diameter, and, using a 3/16-inch V-cone of yellow icing, start each petal at the outer

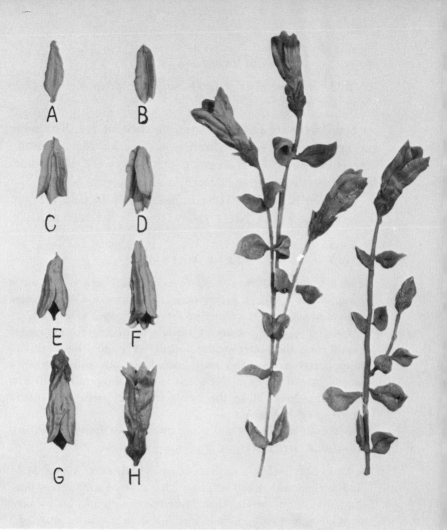

FIGURE 28

edge of the circle and bring it out and away from circle (Fig. 29a). Make two or three rows of overlapping petals that are very irregular in length, angle, and shape.

Fill the center of the flower with chocolate or brown icing, and cover that with No. 2 chocolate or brown dots of icing, or with chocolate nonpareils.

**Add two more rows of petals, slightly overlapping the center
now and then.**

Sunflowers are yellow, brown, or chestnut red. The large
one in Figure 29 is made directly on the cake. Miniature sunflowers can be made on waxed paper on a No. 7 nail, frozen,
removed from paper, and placed in an arrangement.

Children like these. Try putting a funny face on the sunflower center with a No. 2 yellow cone. It is rather startling.

FIELD DAISIES

Fasten a square of waxed paper to a No. 7 nail with a little
icing. With a No. 3 yellow-orange cone make a thin, round
mound of icing on the center of the waxed paper (Fig. 30*a*).

Using a ⅛-inch V-cone of white icing, bring ten or twelve
petals from the center to the outside. (Fig. 30*b*. Be careful to
keep petals narrow and well-tapered at both ends.) Make a
second row of ten or twelve petals between the petals of the first
row (Fig. 30*c*). Make the petals irregular, with some partly
overlapping the others.

Make several daisies and place them in the freezing compartment of a refrigerator for five or ten minutes.

Drop light yellow-green curved stems with a No. 3 cone. Make
bud at right with a ball of green icing covered with yellow dots.
Add short white petals. Then make leaves with a ¼-inch V-cone
of yellow-green icing. (Study special leaf technique on pp. 41 ff.)

Add a mound of green icing with a No. 3 cone wherever a
flower is to be placed in the arrangement. (Fig. 30*d*.)

Remove wax papers from frozen flowers and place them at
different angles on mounds of green icing. Put many No. 2
yellow dots of icing on the centers (Fig. 30*e*), and when the
petals begin to thaw, bend some of them downward.

We selected the field daisy for sentimental reasons. It is

FIGURE 29

the one we always picture in the game of "He loves me; he loves me not." There are many cultivated varieties of daisies and simple chrysanthemums that can be made in a similar way. Colors can be yellow with brown center or yellow, pink, or lavender with yellow center. There are probably still other combinations.

A multitude of asters, coneflowers, bachelor-buttons, and zinnias can also be made with the daisy method.

CHRYSANTHEMUMS

The chrysanthemums pictured here (Fig. 31) are a small-enough variety, 1–1½ inches in diameter, so that they can be made directly on the No. 7 flower nail, removed with a pair of scissors, and placed on the cake immediately.

In this example, however, we used a different method, similar to the one we used for daisies.

Fasten a square of waxed paper to a No. 7 nail with a little icing and make up a cone with a U-shaped No. 81 metal tube and bright-yellow icing.

Keeping the U-tube right side up, start each petal at the outer edge of an imaginary circle (½-inch in diameter) and bring it out and away from the circle as though you were making leaves. Complete the first layer of petals (Fig. 31*a*), then make a second row of petals which mismatches the first row (Fig. 31*b*).

Form a mound of bright-yellow icing in center with a No. 5 cone (Fig. 31*c*). Make as many additional rows of petals as necessary in order to cover the top of the mound completely.

Make five flowers of different sizes and place them in the freezing compartment of a refrigerator for five minutes or more.

Drop a long No. 4 green stem, and draw five short No. 3 stems so that they come out of the long stem at different places.

Make leaves of different sizes and at different angles with a 3/16-inch V-cone. (Study pp. 82–84 for special leaf technique.)

FIGURE 30

Use a few frozen or air-dried leaves (pp. 53 f.) to gain three-dimensional effect.

Form a mound of green icing with a No. 4 cone at the end of each short stem. Remove papers from frozen flowers and place them against mounds at different angles.

Chrysanthemums are white, cream, pink, red, yellow, bronze, and various in-between shades. They vary greatly in size and structure; the next one is one of the largest.

PINCUSHION CHRYSANTHEMUMS

Fasten a 3-inch square of waxed paper to a No. 7 nail with a little icing, and make up a cone with a U-shaped No. 79 metal tube and white icing.

Keep the U-opening of the metal tube in upside-down position for most of the petals. Sometimes use the tube right side up, or on its left or right side in order to gain a variety of petals. Bring some of the petals to a point by pinching the ends between finger and thumb. Use corn starch on your fingers to keep them from becoming sticky.

Start each petal at the outer edge of an imaginary circle ($1/2$-inch in diameter) and bring it out and away from circle as though you were making leaves. Complete the first layer of petals (Fig. 32*a*), and add three more layers of overlapping and irregular petals (Fig. 32*b*).

Using a No. 13 bright-yellow cone, form a mound of icing in the center and cover it with closely packed stars.

Freeze flower for five minutes or more.

Drop a long No. 4 green stem. Make different-sized leaves.

Study pp. 41 ff. for special leaf technique. Notice two very small leaves at base of large leaf at upper right. The large leaf that is arched over the stem is made in a special way that is described on p. 60.

FIGURE 31

FIGURE 32

Make a large ball of green icing at the top of the stem. Remove the waxed paper from the frozen flower and place it against the ball of green icing so that it tilts upward and slightly to one side.

We wish to remind you that miniatures of large flowers can always be made when they are more appropriate. The main thing is to reduce everything in proportion.

The next chapter also deals with leaf-technique flowers, but they are sufficiently different from the others to rate a chapter by themselves.

CHAPTER VII

Deep-Nail Flowers

IN THIS CHAPTER we use a No. 12 deep hollow nail. However, if you wish to make your flowers larger or smaller, you can use any suitable mold, such as a bell or a plastic bell mold, or small wine glass. (See the Easter lilies and the day lilies in the frontispiece.)

We use a No. 70 metal leaf tube that is opened at the center half again as much as normal. However, if you wish to make your flowers larger or smaller, you will have to use a tube of corresponding size.

We also use a cardboard box with 3/4-inch holes in the top as a drying rack. You can easily make one of these out of a pie box or candy box.

To prepare the nail, cut waxed-paper circles 3½ inches in diameter. Cut from edge to center and put shortening (preferably) or icing along right side of cut line (Fig. 33a). Move greased or iced portion of paper to the left and under the rest of the paper to form a cone that will fit the nail. Press cone so that shortening or icing will seal the paper together and hold the cone in shape.

Cut off the point of the cone with scissors so that it will fit the hollow nail better. (Fig. 33b. Save these papers. They can be reused.) Brush the inside of No. 12 deep hollow nail with melted shortening and press the cone of waxed paper against inside of hollow nail.

Using white icing and a No. 70 metal leaf tube that has been opened at the center half again as much as normal, start a tapered leaf at the bottom of the waxed-paper cone. Gradually increase the pressure on the icing as the tube is brought upward against the waxed-paper cone, and gradually decrease pressure on the icing as tube approaches the top edge of the cone (Fig. 33c).

Make two more leaflike petals so that all three are equally spaced (Fig. 33d). Then make three more petals so that they overlap the first three petals except for the top half inch. (Fig. 33e. Be careful to increase pressure considerably at the center of each petal, and do not separate them too far from the top of the cone. Otherwise, they will fall apart later when the paper is removed.)

Lift the cone out of the flower nail and place it in a ¾-inch box hole. Make six or more flowers and place them in the box, and put the rack of flowers in a freezing compartment for ten minutes or in a refrigerator for twenty to thirty minutes. (Do not leave flowers in refrigerator too long. They acquire excess moisture and collapse later at room temperature.)

Then remove papers from frozen flowers and place flowers in box holes again. As soon as flowers thaw enough, point the tips of the petals between thumb and finger and bend tips downward (Fig. 33f).

Put a spot of soft white icing in the bottom of the flower. Make a No. 2 stiff, light yellow-green pistil in center by placing the tip of a tube in the spot of soft white icing, exerting a steady pressure, and bringing tube straight up as far as possible without causing the green icing to collapse.

Make six yellow or amber No. 2 stamens, shorter than the pistil and spaced evenly around it. Brush tops of stamens with a little red color (Fig. 33g).

If you wish to use the Easter lilies immediately in an arrange-

FIGURE 33

ment, freeze them again. Then place the frozen lilies near the
stems and lengthen the base of each flower with a No. 5 cone of
soft white icing. Smooth the spot where flower and bulb work
join with a moist brush or finger.

Brush some very light green color on base near stem. (This method is very much like the one used for petunias, pp. 190–92, and for full nasturtiums, pp. 192–94.)

The method used in Figure 33 and for the flowers in Figure 34 takes longer than the one described above, but it has the advantage of making lilies that stand away from the surface.

After the centers are made, let the flowers air-dry in the box for several hours or overnight. Then take them out of the box and place them upside down in a pan or on a cardboard (Fig. 33*h*). Using a No. 5 cone of soft white icing, lengthen the base of the flower and make it smooth with brush and water. Brush a small amount of light-green color on the base of the lily (Fig. 33*i*).

Allow base to dry for several hours. If lily is to stand vertically from the surface (center one in Figure 34), let base dry overnight.

Drop a No. 5 green main stem (Fig. 34) and add small No. 3 stems for buds and lilies.

Make narrow leaves with ¼-inch V-cone. Then use bulb technique (pp. 33 ff.) and a No. 5 green cone to make the green bud at top right. Make larger white bud at upper right in a similar way.

Place lilies at various angles at the ends of the small stems.

Using a paring knife, make a small cone-shaped hole in the cake. (It should be ¾-inch deep and made in the center of the flower arrangement.) Fill the hole halfway with white decorating icing. Then place the lily firmly in icing so that it stands upright.

Put one or two leaves near the base of the lily to cover the handiwork.

Easter lilies are white, or white tinged with pink. Some kinds have three wide petals alternating with three narrow petals. They resemble the day lily (Fig. 35). Color of centers varies.

Easter lilies are used on Easter cakes and wedding and

FIGURE 34

anniversary cakes. There is no good reason why they can not be used more extensively.

DAY LILIES

Using a No. 70 yellow cone and a No. 12 deep hollow nail, and using a technique similar to that used for Easter lilies (pp. 88 ff., and Fig. 33), make three wide petals (Fig. 35). Then make three narrow petals. (Petals should separate ¾-inch from the top of the waxed-paper cone.)

Make a yellow pistil with No. 2 cone and six yellow stamens with brown tips. Streak the petals with small pointed brush and red vegetable color.

Drop two No. 5 green stems (Fig. 35) and add small No. 3 green stems for lilies and buds. Make wide leaves with a ⅜-inch V-cone, and using bulb technique and No. 5 green cone, make two green buds at top left.

Form a larger yellow bud at top center in a similar way, and place the lilies at various angles on short stems. Place the upright lily near center of the stem arrangement at the right. (Use method described on pp. 90 f. for upright Easter lily in Fig. 34.)

Day lilies and various hybrids of day lilies are tan, yellow, pink, rose, maroon, purple. Some are one color; some are variegated, streaked, or marked in other ways. The colors are especially popular with men and children. They are suitable for almost any gala occasion.

Some have leaves on the stems, as illustrated in Figure 35. Others have long leaves coming out of the ground, similar to the leaves of daffodils (Fig. 63, p. 167).

Use deep-nail flower technique for painted tongue, bluets (Quaker ladies), bellflowers, and delphinium. Add spurs to the latter as for nasturtiums, p. 194.

Study new flowers for differences in shape, color, number of petals, center, arrangement, and greenery. (Seed catalogues are excellent textbooks.) Then try them out with buttercream.

You probably feel that you have enough flowers and flower techniques to keep you busy forever. However, in the next chapter you will learn four basic petals that are the key to making the majority of all buttercream flowers—many more than you have studied up to this point.

FIGURE 35

CHAPTER VIII

The Four Basic Flower Petals

A KNOWLEDGE of the four basic flower petals is essential for making the flowers in the following chapters of this book. In fact, a majority of all flowers can be constructed with these petals and their variations.

You will soon learn to look at a real flower or a good picture of one and to analyze its structure from a cake-decorator's point of view. If it cannot be made with the star, inverted-cone, bulb, or leaf techniques that you have studied so far, you will probably discover that it can be made with variations of one or more of the four basic petals that you will practice while studying this chapter. Sometimes you will find an unusual flower like the snapdragon (pp. 199–203), which combines three of the four basic petals with bulb technique, or the small orchid (pp. 221 f.), which combines leaf technique and two of the four basic petals.

In other words, you are about to learn the rest of the A B C's of flower-making. Just as the letters of the alphabet can be put together to form words, so the elements of flowers can be put together in a boundless variety of combinations.

By learning the rest of your A B C's—the four basic petals —you will understand the instructions in the remainder of this book and will be able to create the flowers for yourself. You will also be able to make the thousands of other flowers that are everywhere in real life and in pictures, and you will be able to analyze and form the new blossoms that appear each year. And you can even create new flowers in buttercream that may not be seen in real life for a thousand years—perhaps never.

Before we begin to practice the basic petals themselves, it is necessary to learn the exact meanings that we shall give to certain terms as they apply to cake decoration.

Basic petals are made with various sizes of straight wedge-shaped metal flower tubes. The base of the tube is the largest part; the top is the smallest part. Be sure that the metal opening forms a perfect wedge before you begin to decorate. The soft metal gets out of shape very easily, but it can just as easily be pressed back into shape between fingers and thumb. If the opening is closed too much, it can be pried apart with a knife, scissors, or a strong pin.

If the double-cone system is used (DC 15 ff.),* be sure that the last third of the metal tube does not contain any paper. Pressure is more evenly controlled if the last third of the tube contains nothing but icing.

Practice all the work in the chapter in the order in which it is discussed. Do not skip around or omit part of it. A clear understanding of the terms will save you a great deal of time. The only way to be sure that you understand a term is to perform the prescribed drill and then compare your work with the illustration; when your work and that illustrated compare favorably, you know that you know.

Use a No. 125 cone for the exercises. Notice hand and cone position in the illustrations—they will help you to visualize the way you should hold your cone when you are practicing the same exercise.

The angle between a vertical line and a horizontal line

---

* "DC" indicates pages in *Decorating Cakes for Fun and Profit;* "27C," pages in *27 Special Creations for Cake Decorators.*

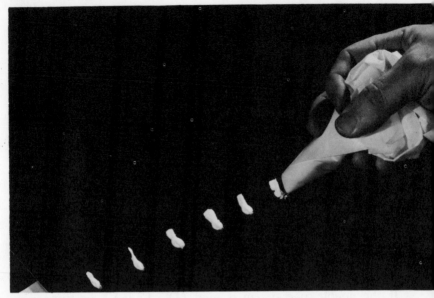

FIGURE 36: LOW-ANGLE PETALS

The base of the tube touches the surface; the top of it almost touches the surface.

(parallel to the top of a cake) is one of 90 degrees. An angle formed by a horizontal line and a line halfway between vertical and horizontal has 45 degrees.

LOW ANGLE (begin at left side of Fig. 36).—Hold the base of the tube at the surface, and keep the top of the tube just off the surface. Press the icing. Then release the pressure. Move the top of the tube downward as you bring the tube away from the icing. (This helps to cut the icing and to give the top edge of the petal a smoother finish.)

Make each petal to the right a little higher than the preceding one.

All of these petals are low, however. The angles vary from 10 to 30 degrees; 45 degrees is considered a medium angle. The space between the metal tube and the surface is the angle

FIGURE 37: HIGH-ANGLE PETALS

The base of the tube touches the surface; the top of it is raised to a point directly above the base.

to which we refer, always—*not* the angle between the paper cone and the surface.

HIGH ANGLE (begin at left side of Fig. 37).—Hold the base of the tube at the surface and keep the top of it off the surface at an angle of 70 degrees (a "high" angle, 25 degrees wider than the medium 45 degrees.)

Press the icing cone until the icing coming out of the tube is fastened to the surface and a complete petal is formed. Stop pressure. (Do not move the base or change the angle of the tube while the petal is being made.) Move the top of the tube downward as you bring the tube away from the icing.

Make each petal to the right a little higher than the preceding one.

In the last petal to the right in Figure 37, the top of the

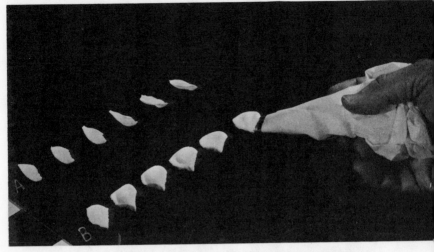

FIGURE 38: TILT-CONE, HIGH-ANGLE PETALS

a) Tilt top of tube to left. Exert pressure.
b) Tilt top of tube to right. Exert pressure.

tube is raised to a point directly above the base of the tube. This is a 90-degree angle—the space between the horizontal line along the surface and the vertical line of the metal-tube opening.

TILT CONE, I (begin at left side of Fig. 38*a*).—Hold the base of the tube at the surface. Keep the top of the tube raised to a point directly above the base of the tube. (This is the highest, or 90-degree, angle.)

Tilt the top of the tube (and the entire cone and hand) a little to the left. Press the icing in the tube. (But do not move the base or change the angle or tilt of the tube while the petal is being formed.)

Release pressure after the petal is thoroughly fastened to the surface and is completely formed. Move the top of the tube downward as you bring the tube away from the petal and toward you.

Tilt each succeeding petal a little more to the left.

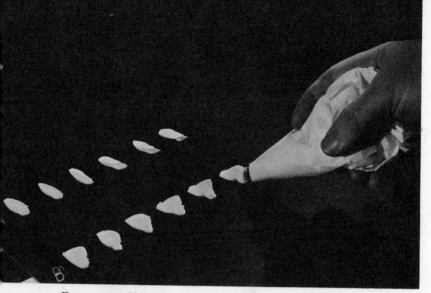

FIGURE 39: TILT-&-STRAIGHTEN HIGH-ANGLE PETALS

a) Tilt to left; exert pressure.
b) Tilt to left; exert pressure. Release pressure, and keep high angle as the cone is straightened.

II (begin at left side of Fig. 38*b*).—Hold the base of the tube at the surface, and keep the top of the tube raised to a point directly above the base of the tube. Tilt the top of the tube (and the entire cone and hand) a little to the right. Press the icing. (Do not move the base or change the angle or tilt of the tube while the petal is being formed.)

Release pressure after the petal is thoroughly fastened to the surface and is completely formed. Move the top of the tube downward as you bring it away from the petal and toward you.

Tilt each succeeding petal a little more to the right.

TILT AND STRAIGHTEN (begin at left side of Fig. 39*b*).—To make six petals at high angle and left tilt, make a petal as in Figure 39*a*, releasing the pressure after the petal is completely formed.

Keep the base against the surface, and keep the tube at a high angle as the cone is straightened—that is, the metal tube again forms a vertical line to the horizontal surface as it did before it was tilted (Fig. 39*b*, at extreme right).

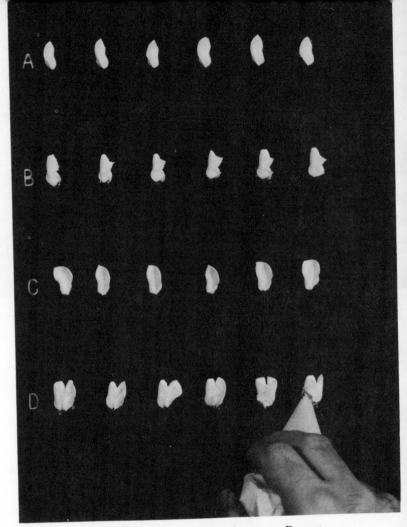

FIGURE 40: LOW-ANGLE OVERLAP PETALS

a) Cone at low angle, with left tilt. Exert pressure.
b) Tilt low-angle cone to left; exert pressure. Then release pressure and straighten cone.
c) Tilt cone to right, then exert pressure.
d) Tilt cone to right; exert pressure and continue it, keeping the base of the tube against the surface and the tube at a right angle. Then give tube a left tilt. Release pressure, and bring the top of the tube down to the surface.

This forms a cupped petal that opens to the right. If a right-tilted petal is straightened, a cupped petal that opens to the left is formed. Continue the exercise:

Move the top of the tube downward as you bring the tube away from the petal and toward you.

Tilt and straighten the rest of the petals (Fig. 39b).

OVERLAP PETALS.—Practice several 20-degree low-angled left-tilt petals (Fig. 40a).

Straighten several 20-degree-angled left-tilt petals so that they cup to the right (Fig. 40b). Do not finish these petals in the usual way; bring the tube away to the right without bringing the top of it downward toward the base of the petal.

Practice several 20-degree-angled right-tilt petals (Fig. 40c).

Straighten six 20-degree-angled left-tilt petals so that they cup to the right. Finish them as in Figure 40b.

Make a 20-degree-angled right-tilt petal to the right of the first petal in Figure 40d. (Place the base of the tube at the base of the left petal previously made before making the right-tilt petal. When the right-tilt petal is being formed, make sure that the icing touches the bottom edge of the first petal.)

Begin another 20-degree-angled right-tilt petal to the right of the second petal in Figure 40d, but continue pressure as you increase the angle of the tube and petal to 45 degrees.

Begin another 20-degree-angled right-tilt petal to the right of the third petal in Figure 40d, but continue pressure as you raise the angle of the tube and petal to 90 degrees.

Begin another 20-degree-angled right-tilt petal to the right of the fourth petal in Figure 40d. Continue pressure as you raise the angle of the tube and petal to 90 degrees; then continue pressure as you straighten the petal so that the top of the tube is directly above the base of the tube.

Begin another 20-degree-angled right-tilt petal to the right of the fifth petal in Figure 40*d*; continue pressure as you raise the angle of the tube to 90 degrees, straighten petal, and then continue pressure as you give the tube a medium left tilt.

Make another petal like the last one to the right of the sixth petal in Figure 40*d*. Release pressure. Move the top of the tube downward and fasten the icing to the petal at the left (Fig. 40*d*, last part to right). Finally, bring the tube away from both petals and toward you.

Notice that the final result is a bud or flower center made up of two low-angled petals that are cupped toward each other, with one overlapping the other. After a little practice you can make the right petal overlap the left one in one smooth, uninterrupted movement.

[1] THE SIMPLE CENTER PETAL

This is the first of the four basic petals. If you have studied and practiced the preceding exercises, you will find the next ones easy and enjoyable.

The term "simple" in the title denotes the fact that the base of the tube does not move from its original position, no matter how the tube is angled or tilted (an exception being found, though, in Fig. 41*k*). The term "center" is used because this kind of petal very commonly (but not always) occurs at the center of a flower.

Practice the following exercises carefully. Refer to the preceding practice pages when the results of your efforts do not compare favorably with those illustrated. This work will give you a new confidence in your ability to make the exact petal you want when you want it.

(The letters in parentheses at the beginning of paragraphs refer to letters identifying parts of the accompanying illustration, in each case.)

FIGURE 41.—(*a*) Make two pairs of low-angled no-tilt petals. Keep the base of the tube in the same spot when making both petals of the same pair. (These are often used in making flower buds.)

(*b*) Make two pairs of low-angled, extremely tilted petals.

Keep the base of the tube in the same spot when making both petals of the same pair, as before. Choose the angle first, then choose the tilt. Do not move the tube from that position until the petal is completely formed and pressure is released. After the pressure is released for each petal, bringing the top of the tube downward, away from the icing and toward you, helps to cut the icing from the tube and gives the edge of the petal a smoother finish.

(*c*) Make two pairs of low-angled extremely tilted and straightened petals.

Do not move the base of the tube, even though the top of it is angled, tilted, then straightened at the same angle. Do not straighten the petal until it is completely formed and pressure is released. Do not bring the tube away from the petal until pressure is released and the top of the tube is brought downward.

(*d*) Make two pairs of low-angled, extremely tilted over-lapping petals. (Review detailed description on pp. 101 f.)

(*e*) Make one pair of medium-angled, medium-tilted petals. Then make another pair of medium-angled petals that are tilted more than the first pair.

(*f*) Make two pairs of medium-angled, medium-tilted straightened petals.

(*g*) Make a pair of high-angled, extremely tilted petals. (After the pressure is released, give a smooth finish to the edge of a near-horizontal petal by moving the top of the tube toward the base of the petal as the tube is brought away from the icing and toward you.)

(*h*) Make a pair of high-angled, extremely tilted straightened petals.

(*i*) Make two pairs of high-angled, medium left-tilted straightened petals.

Both petals are tilted to the left before they are straightened. Notice that both petals are cupped to the right.

(*j*) Make two pairs of high-angled, medium right-tilted straightened petals.

Both petals are tilted to the right before they are straightened. Notice that both petals are cupped to the left.

(*k*) Make a single high-angled, extremely left-tilted straightened petal. Then make another petal just like it but place it so that it will become the right member of the pair in the illustration.

Now place the base of the tube ½ inch to the *left* of the petal just made, giving the tube a high angle and an extreme *right* tilt. Move the base to the right and the top to the left as the petal is formed.

Move the base of the tube until it touches the base of the petal to the right. Notice that the petals cup away from each other.

(*l*) Make a high-angled, medium left-tilted petal. Join to it a medium-angled, extremely right-tilted straightened petal. Then make another pair just like this pair.

(*m*) Make two pairs of high-angled no-tilt petals with a narrow V position to each other.

Notice that the left petal is pointed slightly to the left and the right petal slightly to the right. The base of the tube is kept at the same point for both petals.

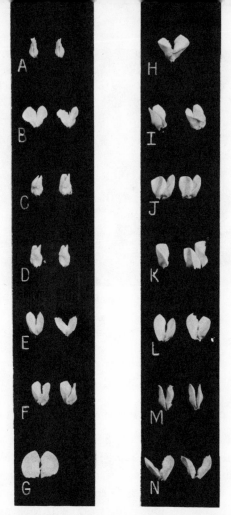

FIGURE 41: SIMPLE CENTER PETALS

Low angle: (*a*) no tilt; (*b*) extreme tilt; (*c*) extreme tilt, straighten;
   (*d*) extreme tilt, straighten left petal, overlap right petal.

Medium angle: (*e*) medium tilt; (*f*) medium tilt, straighten.

High angle: (*g*) extreme tilt; (*h*) extreme tilt, straighten; (*i*) both
   petals left tilt, straighten both petals; (*j*) both petals right tilt,
   straighten both petals.

k) Right petal: high angle, extreme left tilt, straighten. Left petal:
   high angle, extreme right tilt. Place the base of the tube ¼ inch
   to the left of the first petal; move the base to the right and the
   top to the left as the petal is formed.

l) Left petal: high angle, medium tilt. Right petal: medium angle,
   extreme tilt, straighten.

V formations: (*m*) narrow; (*n*) wide.

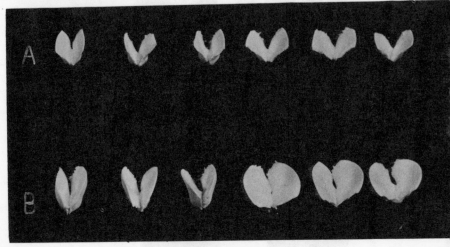

FIGURE 42: MATCHED PETALS
a) Both low-angle, same degree of tilt.
b) Both high-angle, same degree of tilt.

(*n*) Make two pairs of high-angled, slightly tilted petals with a wide V position to each other.

MATCHED AND UNMATCHED PETALS

Before studying the rest of the basic petals, it will be well to realize fully not only that there is an infinite variety of flower petals but that there is also an infinite number of ways in which petals can be combined. Then we will never make flowers one too much like another. Our work will look more natural because no two flowers, nor any two of anything else in the universe (including cake-decorators), are exactly alike.

In the next exercise you will find that it is easier to make matched petals than to make unmatched ones. Of course, if you study Figures 42 and 43 closely, you will see that no two petals are *exactly* alike; even so-called matched petals are not the same, though they seem so at first glance. This gives a clue to why there is so much sameness in the decorations on many cakes. It is easier to repeat an old action automatically than to think of and initiate a new one. However, work that is too similar is machinelike, unnatural.

As you practice matched petals (those that are similar) and unmatched petals (those that are dissimilar), you will be training yourself to think about the many ways in which variety can be obtained. Your work will become more and more natural—and interesting—as a result. Of course, you must also use some matched petals to promote the natural appearance of your work, for many flowers in nature appear identical with others of their kind.

MATCHED (Fig. 42).—(*a*) Make three sets of matched petals with low angle and slight tilt. Then make three sets of matched petals with low angle and greater tilt.

(*b*) Make three sets of matched petals with high angle and slight tilt. Then make three sets of matched petals with high angle and extreme tilt.

UNMATCHED (Fig. 43).—(*a*) Make six sets of unmatched petals, using a low angle for each left petal of a pair and a high angle for each right petal, and the same medium tilt for both.

(*b*) Make six sets of unmatched petals, using a medium tilt for petals on the left and an extreme tilt for those on the right, and the same high angle for both.

(*c*) Make six sets of unmatched petals, using a high angle and no tilt for petals on the left and a low angle and an extreme tilt for those on the right.

Make up other matched and unmatched petal combinations of your own. You will never run out of possible variations; and you will never get tired of cake-decorating, because you can always do something new.

This, the second of the four basic flower petals, you will find to be exactly what its name implies—a simple center petal that is extended upward from the surface and forward from its starting point. (Alphabetic letters, as before, refer to lettered details in the illustration.)

FIGURE 44.—(*a*) Hold the tube at a high angle and medium left tilt. Form a simple center petal but do not release pressure or remove tube.

(*b*) Maintain the pressure as before and lift the tube straight up along a vertical line until the base of the tube is 1/4 inch off the surface.

(*c*) Maintain the original pressure and move the tube straight forward 1/4 inch along a line horizontal to the surface.

(*d*) Still maintaining the same pressure, move the tube straight back for 1/4 inch on the same horizontal line that was used in *c* above.

(*e*) Maintain the same pressure at first but gradually reduce it as you bring the tube straight down along a 1/4-inch vertical line to the original starting point in *a* above.

The formula for the extended-center petal is "pressure" (to form the simple center petal)—then "up, forward, back, and down" (Fig. 44*f*). (Fig. 44*g* gives a side view of the five steps *a–e* above.)

If the petal collapses, the trouble may be due to a number of things. Check the following:

Icing too soft

Simple center petal not formed completely before tube was lifted off surface

Tube lifted more than 1/4 inch

Tube moved forward more than 1/4 inch

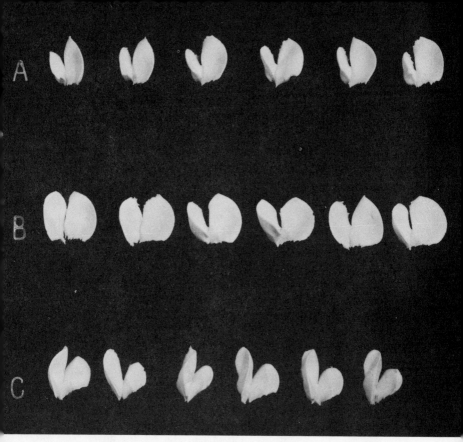

FIGURE 43: UNMATCHED PETALS

a) Each left petal at low angle, right petal at high angle; same medium tilt for both.

b) Left petal at medium tilt, right petal at extreme tilt; same high angle for both.

c) Left petal at high angle, with no tilt; right petal at low angle, with extreme tilt.

Tube moved back more than ¼ inch

Tube not brought down to original starting point of petal

Too much pressure on the icing in the tube at any one or all of the various stages

Too little pressure on the icing at any one or all of the stages

If, on the other hand, the petal appears too heavy, too thick, or too wide, check the following:

Icing too soft

Simple center petal formed with too much icing before the tube was lifted from the surface

Tube not lifted high enough or moved forward far enough

Too much pressure on the icing in the tube at any one or all of the various stages

Tube moved forward and up on a diagonal line instead of up on a vertical line and then forward on a horizontal line

Tube moved back and down on a diagonal line instead of back on a horizontal line and down on a vertical line

The extended-center petal is as light and delicate as a real flower petal when it is properly made. Learn to make it well before you practice the following variations.

FIGURE 44.—(*h*) Make a left extended-center petal at a high angle with a medium-left tilt. Then make a right extended-center petal at a high angle with a medium-right tilt.

(*i*) Make both petals as in *h*, but straighten them.

(*j*) Make both petals of the first flower at a high angle with no tilt. Then make both petals of the second flower at a high angle with a slight tilt.

(*k*) Make the left petal of the first flower at a high angle with a left tilt, and straighten. Then make the right petal of that flower at a high angle and a right tilt. (Do *not* straighten.)

Make both petals of the second flower as in the first, but make them in a narrower V position to each other.

(*l*) Make both petals in each flower at a medium angle with a medium tilt, and straighten.

This angle is used for buds. To make buds with extended-center petals, it is very important to keep the pressure to a minimum and to shorten the vertical and horizontal extensions. Otherwise the petals will be too heavy.

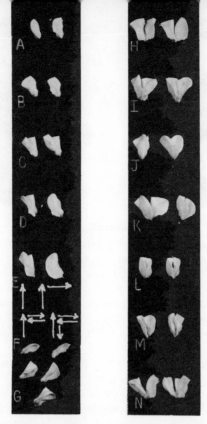

FIGURE 44: EXTENDED-CENTER PETALS

a) At a high angle, with medium left tilt, form a simple center petal.

b) Continue same pressure as in *a*. Lift tube off the surface ¼ inch straight up.

c) Continue same pressure. Move the tube straight forward ¼ inch.

d) Continue same pressure. Move tube straight back ¼ inch along same line as in *c*.

e) Gradually reduce the pressure, and bring the tube straight down ¼ inch to the original starting point.

f) The formula for the extended center petal: *Pressure . . . then up; forward; back; down.*

g) Side views of the five steps shown in *a-e*.

h) Extended-center petals, at high angle, with (*left*) medium left tilt and (*right*) medium right tilt.

i) Same as *h*, but both petals straightened.

j) Both petals at high angle, no tilt.

k) High-angle petals: (*left*) left tilt, straighten; (*right*) right tilt.

l) Both made at medium angle, medium tilt; straighten.

m) Narrow V formation.

n) Wide V formation.

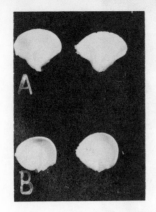

FIGURE 45: SIMPLE BACK PETAL

a) With cone at low angle, with extreme right tilt, bend the wrist inward. Pivot on the base of the tube while gradually increasing, then gradually decreasing, pressure on tube. Keep the low angle and extreme right tilt until pressure is completely relaxed.

b) With cone at high angle, at extreme right tilt, bend the wrist inward and pivot, as in *a*.

c) Same as *a*, but move the top of the tube slightly up and down to make folds.

d) Same as *a*, but with the cone at a higher angle toward the end of the pivoting, to produce a tilted petal.

(*m*) Make high-angled extended-center petals in a narrow V position to each other.

(*n*) Make high-angled extended-center petals in a wide V position.

[III] THE SIMPLE BACK PETAL

This is the third of the four basic petals. Just as in the case of the simple center petal (pp. 102 ff.), the term "simple" denotes the fact that the base of the tube does not move from its original position, no matter how the tube is angled or tilted. The term "back" is used because this type of petal very commonly (but not always) occurs at the "back" of a flower, near the stem.

Practice the following exercises carefully so that you will be able to make the flowers in succeeding chapters more easily.

When the results of your efforts do not compare favorably with those shown in the illustration, refer to the instructions for holding and tilting the tube at the beginning of this chapter.

FIGURE 45.—(*a*) Touch the base of the tube lightly but steadily at one point on the surface and hold it there while a complete petal is being formed. Keep the tube at a low angle and an extreme right tilt.

Bend your wrist inward toward your body so that pivoting motion will be easier. Pivot the base of the tube against the surface while gradually increasing and then decreasing the pressure on the icing in the tube. Keep a low angle and an extreme right tilt until the pressure on the icing is released completely.

Tilt the top of the tube toward the pivot base of the petal and bring the tube toward that pivot base and toward you.

This last motion will give the bottom right edge of the petal a smooth finish. Watch out for the following:

Do not push the base of the tube into the surface. Just pivot it lightly as the petal is being made.

Do not press the icing first and then pivot the tube. Pivot the tube and press the icing at the same time.

Do not use too much pressure on the icing at first. Gradually increase the pressure at first and then gradually decrease it toward the end.

Do not finish the petal at a different angle and tilt unless you intend to make it look like that result (Fig. 45*d*). Keep tilt and angle the same from beginning to end.

Do not keep pressure on the icing when you bring the tube away from the completed petal. Release the pressure compeltely before you bring the tube away.

Do not bring the tube away at just any angle. Tilt the top of

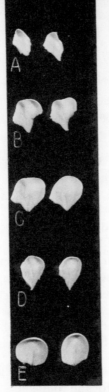

FIGURE 46: EXTENDED-BACK PETAL

a) Low angle, extreme right tilt. Bend wrist inward. Keep base of tube against surface. Gradually increase pressure on icing as base of tube is moved straight forward one-fourth inch.

b) Continue same pressure as in A. Pivot tube on base as for simple back petal.

c) Keep base of tube against surface. Keep low angle, extreme right tilt. Gradually decrease pressure on icing, and bring base of tube back down the original straight one-fourth inch line to starting point.

d) Repeat A, B, and C, but pivot one-half as much.

e) Repeat A, B, and C, but use high angle.

f) Repeat A, B, and C, but move top of tube slightly up and down to form folds.

g) Repeat A, B, and C, but move whole tube continuously back and forth to form ridges.

h) Repeat A, B, and C, but use higher angle toward end of pivoting motion, producing a tilted petal.

i) Repeat A, B, and C, but use a high angle at first and a lower angle toward end of pivoting motion, producing a tilted petal.

j) Repeat A, B, and C, but extend petal three-fourths inch instead of one-fourth inch.

it toward the pivot center of the petal and bring it toward that center and toward you.

(*b*) Give the tube a high angle and an extreme right tilt. Bend your wrist inward toward your body, and pivot the tube as in *a*, above, and press the icing at the same time. (Study the list of precautions above and the instructions given for Fig. 45*a*, above.)

(*c*) Holding the tube as in *a*, above, use pressure on the icing and pivot the tube in the same way, but move the top of the tube slightly up and down to form folds of icing.

(*d*) Make the same petal as in *a*, above, but use a higher angle toward the end of the pivoting motion, to produce a tilted petal.

[IV] THE EXTENDED-BACK PETAL

This last of the four basic petals is a simple back petal that is extended forward for a quarter of an inch, more or less, along the surface. Since it is extended horizontally only, it is much easier to make than the extended-center petal (pp. 108–112), which is extended horizontally and vertically.

(Letters in parentheses in the following instructions indicate, as before, lettered details of the illustration.)

FIGURE 46.—(*a*) Hold the tube at a low angle and an extreme right tilt, and bend your wrist inward. Keeping the base of the tube against the surface, gradually increase the pressure on the icing in the tube as the base of the tube is moved straight forward ¼ inch.

(*b*) Maintaining the same pressure as in *a*, pivot the base of the tube against the surface, as for a simple back petal (Fig. 45*a*).

(*c*) Keeping the base of the tube against the surface, at a low angle and with an extreme right tilt, gradually decrease the pressure on the icing and bring the base of the tube back down the original, straight ¼-inch line to the starting point. Release pressure.

Dip the top of the tube toward the base of the petal, and bring the tube toward the base of the petal and toward you to give a smooth finish to the bottom right side of the petal.

(*d*) Repeat *a–c*, above, but pivot only half as much, to get a narrower petal.

(*e*) Repeat *a–c*, above, but use a high angle to cup the petal.

(*f*) Repeat *a–c*, above, but move the top of the tube slightly up and down to form folds or waves. (Do not lift the base of the tube off the surface.)

(*g*) Repeat *a–c*, above, but move the entire tube continuously and alternately forward and backward a distance of 1/16 inch to form ridges. (Do not lift the base of the tube off the surface while it is being moved back and forth.)

(*h*) Repeat *a–c*, above, but use a higher angle toward the end of the pivoting motion, to produce a tilted petal.

(*i*) Repeat *a–c*, above, but use a high angle at first and a lower angle toward the end of the pivoting motion, to produce a different tilt to the petal.

(*j*) Repeat *a–c*, above, but extend the petal ¾ inch instead of ¼ inch before pivoting, to produce a much longer petal.

We shall put these four basic petals and their numberless variations and possible combinations to good use in making all the flowers in the chapters that follow. We hope that you will also put them to good use in imitating other flowers that you see in nature and in pictures. And do not hesitate to imagine a few others, and to create them, too.

CHAPTER IX

Direct Basic-Petal Flowers

THE FLOWERS in this chapter can be made directly on a cake by using one or more of the four basic petals (Chapter VIII). Some of them can also be made on a metal surface, frozen, removed with a sharp knife, and placed in an arrangement.

VETCHES

Vetches grow on vines that climb around fences and other objects and cling to them by means of tendrils at the ends of their leaf stems (Fig. 47).

Drop a long, graceful double-curved No. 4 green stem from the upper right to the lower left corner of the arrangement. Then drop two curved No. 3 green stems above the main stem, and two more below it. Make two scroll-like No. 2 green tendrils at the end of each leaf stem.

Using a No. 104 wedge-shaped flower tube with blue icing and a medium angle (p. 96) and no tilt (p. 103), make two simple center petals (pp. 102 ff.) in a very narrow V formation (p. 104) ⅛ inch from the stem (they look like sweet-pea buds) putting one flower (two petals) at the end of each of the two flower stems. Mismatch six flowers down each side of both stems.

Join flowers to stems with two or three green sepals made with a No. 3 green cone and by leaf-pressure technique (DC 29, 39 f.).

Make two narrow green leaves with a ⅛-inch V-cone at the point where each leaf or flower stem comes out of the main stem. Then, using a ¼-inch V-cone of green icing and horizontal leaf technique (pp. 43 f.), make narrow, smooth, long-tapered leaves placed opposite each other, ten on each side of a stem. Have a few overlap others and some of the flowers. Make them at various angles and tilt them in different ways to give naturalness to the arrangement.

Vetches are lavender, purple, blue, or white. This vine makes a beautiful design on the top or on the side of a cake, and it can also be used on both the top and the side of the same cake. In that case, except for a border at the base, no other decoration would be needed.

You might make a fence on the top or side of a cake and wind the vines around it.

WISTERIA

Wisteria grow on vines that often hang from arbors (Fig. 48). The clusters of flowers resemble bunches of grapes. The flower stems and leaf stems are separate but all come out of the main vine. (The step-by-step method is illustrated upside down at the left in order to show more clearly how the clusters of flowers are made with buttercream icing.)

Holding a No. 104 white cone at a 45-degree angle, make an S-shaped mound of icing that is small at the top and large at the bottom (Fig. 48*a*).

Using the No. 104 white cone at a medium high angle (p. 97) and with a slight tilt (p. 106), make a pair of straightened extended-center petals (pp. 108–112) in a narrow V formation (p. 104) at the top of the mound of icing (Fig. 48*a*). Now make two more pairs of the same petals just below (but not touching) the first pair, but do not make them in a straight line (Fig. 48*b*).

Avoid making this second row and succeeding rows of flowers in straight horizontal lines. Make flowers to the left of the center point upward to the left; make those to the right of the center point upward to the right. The ones in the center can face straight ahead or a little to left or right.

Figure 47

Next, make three more pairs of the same or similar petals just touching the row above (Fig. 48c), *varying angle and tilt* of petals and combining them differently to give a natural effect. Make four more pairs of similar petals that touch the row above (Fig. 48d), then five more pairs that touch that row above (Fig. 48e). Finally, make three more pairs of similar petals that fill in the hollow space at the bottom of the cluster (Fig. 48f).

Drop a No. 4 green main stem at the top of the arrangement (Fig. 48) and two long No. 3 green stems from the main stem, with one short stem between them.

Using a ⅜-inch V-cone, make smooth, well-tapered leaves at ends and at both sides of leaf stems. (Study pp. 41 ff. for variations in leaf-making.) Make a cluster of wisteria at the end of the small stem (Figs. 48a–f).

When wisteria hang down, they are right side up—contradictory as that may seem. Wisteria are pink, violet, or white and can be used as top or side decoration.

Represent an upright or overhead trellis and have them hang from that. Or represent a window scene (from the inside looking out), with wisteria across the top and at one corner of the window.

(Remember that flowers can always be made in miniature with smaller tubes, to fit your design.)

SWEET PEAS

Sweet peas also climb by means of tendrils. They look like little corkscrews in the arrangement to the right in Figure 49. The flowers in this arrangement are annuals, with center petals large and full. Perennials, having smaller center petals, are pictured in the next to the top row at the left. (The first two rows deal with the perennial type of sweet pea.)

FIGURE 48

FIGURE 49

Using a No. 125 white cone, make a large, wavy extended-back petal (pp. 115 f.) with a slight dip near top center (Fig. 49*a*). Make two large wavy extended-back petals, one on top of the other. (Fig. 49*b*). This is the way to start a double sweet pea. The rest of it is made the same as the single variety.)

Make a large, wavy extended-back petal. Then place the base of tube at the base of the extended-back petal and, pointing it straight forward, form a simple center petal (pp. 102 ff.) at a low angle (p. 96) with no tilt (p. 103 and Fig. 49*c*).

Make a large back petal as before, and form a pair of simple center petals like that in Figure 49*c* so that they cup toward each other and close together (Fig. 49*d*).

Repeat the petals in Figure 49*d*. Put the base of the tube at the base of the flower and point the tube to the left. Make a high-angled, medium left-tilted simple center petal (Fig. 49*e*).

Make petals as in Figure 49*e*. Put the base of the tube at the base of the flower and point the tube to the right. Make a high-angled, medium right-tilted simple center petal (Fig. 49*f*).

Now make petals as in Figure 49*f*, but for the last two petals place the base of the tube at either side of the two low-angled petals before making them (Fig. 49*g*). Finally make a large, wavy extended-back petal, using a narrow V formation to make a pair of high-angled, slightly-tilted straightened simple center petals that cup together (Fig. 49*h*).

In this case, the two low-angled petals formed for previous flowers are not made, because they are not visible in the final flower. The next two rows deal with the annual type of sweet pea:

Repeat the large extended-back petal (Fig. 49*i*). Then repeat the large extended-back petal and add one low-angled simple center petal (Fig. 49*j*). Repeat the large extended-back petal and add *two* low-angled simple center petals so that they cup toward each other and close together (Fig. 49*k*).

Now repeat petals in Figure 49*k*; placing the base of the tube at the base of the flower, tilt the tube to the left at a very high angle and make an extended-center petal (pp. 108–112 and Fig. 49*l*). Repeat petals in Figure 49*l*; place the base of the tube at the base of the flower and tilt the tube to the right at a very high angle and make an extended-center petal (Fig. 49*m*).

Make a large wavy extended-back petal. Using a narrow V formation, make a pair of high-angled, no-tilt extended-center petals that cup together. (Fig. 49*n*. In this case the two low-angled petals formed for previous flowers are not made, because they are not visible in the final flower.)

Repeat the petals in Figure 49*m*, but tilt the extended-center petals to the extreme left and right (Fig. 49*o*); then repeat petals of Figure 49*m* but tilt the left extended-center petal to the extreme left and the right one only slightly to the right (Fig. 49*p*).

The fifth row shows how sweet-pea buds can be made at different stages by using simple center and simple back petals:

Make two very low-angled (10-degree) no-tilt simple center petals that are kept close together (Fig. 49*q*) and, after that, two low-angled (20-degree) no-tilt simple center petals that are cupped closely together (Fig. 49*r*). Next make a narrow simple back petal (pp. 112–15) and add two low-angled (30-degree) slightly tilted simple center petals that are straightened and cupped toward each other (Fig. 49*s*).

Make a wide simple back petal. Add the very low-angled petals in Figure 49*q*. Add two medium-angled, slightly tilted straightened simple center petals to the left and the right of the very low-angled petals at bottom center (Fig. 49*t*).

The sixth row shows how larger sweet-pea buds can be made at different stages by using short extended-center and short extended-back petals:

Cup together a pair of low-angled (25-degree), no-tilt, short extended-center petals (Fig. 49*u*). Then make a narrow, short extended-back petal and add a pair of low-angled (30-degree), slightly tilted, straightened, short extended-center petals that are cupped toward each other (Fig. 49*v*). Make a short extended-back petal and add the simple very low-angled petals in Figure 49*q*. Add two medium-angled, slightly tilted, straightened short extended-center petals to left and right of the very low-angled petals at bottom center (Fig. 49*w*).

The last row shows some variations of the annual variety of sweet pea. Notice that the very low-angled simple center petals are omitted in the first three examples because the extended-center petals are made in such a way that the simple petals would not be visible in the completed flowers.

Make a wide, wavy extended-back petal that dips slightly at the top center. Add two high-angled, medium-tilted, straightened extended-center petals that cup away from each other (p. 112 and Fig. 49*x*).

Make a back petal as in Figure 49*x*, and then two high-angled, medium-tilted, straightened extended-center petals that cup to the right (p. 110 and Fig. 49*y*). Make a back petal as in Figure 49*x*, and two high-angled, medium-tilted, straightened extended-center petals that cup to the left (p. 110 and Fig. 49*z*).

Make a back petal as in Figure 49*x*. Make two very low-angled simple center petals that are cupped closely together at the base of the back petal. Add two very high-angled, extremely-tilted extended-center petals to left and right of the very low-angled petals at bottom center. (Fig. 49*aa*. Do not straighten extended center petals.)

In making the spray arrangement to the right, drop three No. 3 green stems according to basic principles in DC 58 *ff*. and add annual variety of sweet peas of different sizes and shapes. (If stems break, cut them with two edges of a flower tube, then make a flower just above the open space. Sepals cover open space in stem.)

Make two or three sepals of various sizes and shapes at the base of each flower, using a No. 3 green cone and leaf-pressure technique (DC 29, 39 f.). Using same cone and pressure technique or ⅛-inch V-cone, make leaves. Then make tendrils with a very fine paper-cone opening and roping technique (DC 66).

Sweet peas are white, cream, pink, red, lavender, blue-purple, and intermediate colors. Turn the arrangement around for a different effect, and try other arrangements (DC 57 ff.), using sweet peas or some of the other flowers you have learned or will learn.

Make two dozen sweet peas on a metal surface and freeze them for four or five minutes. Remove them with a sharp knife and air dry them on cardboard for an hour or two, or overnight.

Put a small piece of cake on top of a cake surface and cover the piece with light-green icing. Then cover the piece of iced cake with a mound of air-dried sweet peas in various pastel shades. Draw a few stems from the bottom so that the arrangement looks like a thick bouquet.

Omit the air-drying step if you wish. Place the frozen flowers directly on cake and, as soon as they begin to thaw, curve petals that are too straight.

3-D ROSES

As you have probably guessed, the term "3-D roses" means three-dimensional roses. We use the term to distinguish these from the nail roses, which are also three-dimensional (DC 49 ff.).* While each nail rose is formed completely on a small turntable called a flower nail and is then removed from the nail and placed on a cake, 3-D roses are made directly against a cake surface or on a metal surface, using the basic

---

* "DC" indicates pages in *Decorating Cakes for Fun and Profit;* "27C," pages in *27 Special Creations for Cake Decorators.*

petals. Usually, a rose made in this manner is called a half-rose because it more nearly resembles half a rose than a whole one. The 3-D rose, however, is a whole rose made in a direct fashion without the use of a flower nail.

We are the first to admit the good points of the nail rose, but we also wish to stress the good points of the 3-D rose. When roses are used in a reclining position—as in sprays, corsages with stems showing, or wreaths—3-D roses are especially appropriate. Nail roses can also be used in such arrangements, but they have to be made and trimmed carefully at the base. 3-D roses can be made more quickly than nail roses. Also, it is difficult and sometimes impossible to make buttercream nail roses stay on the side of a cake, while 3-D buttercream roses can be formed directly onto the side of a cake.

Regardless of the advantages and disadvantages of the nail and 3-D roses, most decorators will agree that it is best to be versatile and to know both techniques. Before you study the exercises below, let us note that the bottom petals of a reclining rose are closer to the center than the top petals. The weight of the flower rests on the lowest petals; the top petals are not weighed down at all.

Make a narrow extended-back petal with a No. 125 white cone. (Fig. 50*a*. It is good practice to put a few waves in the extended-back and center petals of roses that are open to any degree. Small buds like those in Figures 50*k-m* should have smooth petals.)

Starting the base of the tube at the base of the first petal, make a second narrow extended-back petal on top of the first petal, but begin it to the right of center. (Fig. 50*b*. The second petal should overlap to the right of the first one. Do not put one directly above the other.)

Place the base of the tube below the surface of previous petals so that the top of the tube is even with the top edge of the flower, or slightly below it.

Using a low angle and a medium left tilt, make a simple center petal and straighten it so that it cups to the right. Now stop pressure: do *not* finish the petal in usual manner, but bring the tube away to the right without dipping the top of the tube downward toward the base of petal (Fig. 50*c*). Placing the base of tube below surface of previous petals and using a very low angle and an extreme right tilt, overlap the first petal with a second petal that is similar (Fig. 50*d*; study detailed technique for overlap petal on pp. 101–102).

Now placing the base of the tube to the *right* of the base of flower, point the tube and cone toward a place to the *left* of the overlapped petals and near the top of the flower. Make a high-angled extended-center petal that is tilted slightly to the right (Fig. 50*e*). Placing the base of the tube to the *left* of the base of the flower, point the tube and cone toward a place to the *right* of the overlapped petals and near the top of the flower.

For the second extended-center petal that is about to be made, omit the pressure that is ordinarily used before the extended-center petal is brought up, forward, back, and down. The first extended petal in Figure 50*e* will support the second one adequately. This maneuver reduces the amount of icing at the center of the rose and makes it more delicate.

After placing the tube in proper position, make a second high-angled extended-center petal that is tilted slightly to the left (Fig. 50*f*). Placing the base of the tube at the center of the base of the flower, make an extended-back petal formed in a nearly vertical position. (Fig. 50*g*. Make certain that the base of the tube travels straight up and down on the same vertical 1/4-inch line. The base of the petal must end at the same point at which it began.)

Figure 50*h* shows the rose turned around and facing us; it is usually more attractive in this position. The third and

FIGURE 50

fourth rows in the illustration show how roses may be made in various stages of development.

Hold the tube at a very low angle (10 degrees or less) with no tilt and press icing (Fig. 50*i*). Crowd green sepals closely around the rose so that just a bit of color shows at the top. It will look like a green bud just starting to open. (Sepals are shown in three arrangements, but not in Figure 50*i*).

Make two very low-angled overlapped simple center petals (pp. 102 ff. and Fig. 50*j*). Put green sepals against it (but let more of the flower show than would be the case in Figure 50*i*). Now make a narrow simple back petal and two 35-degree-angled overlapped simple center petals (Fig. 50*k*).

Put part of the green sepals against it and part of them down over the receptacle and the stem below. The sepals in the rest of the steps are apt to be like this; sometimes all of them will be down over the receptacle and near or against the stem.

Make a wide simple back petal. Then make two 35-degree-angled overlapped simple center petals, and place two more simple center petals in the same position as the two extended-center petals in Figure 50*f* (Fig. 50*l*). Overlap two simple back petals just as the two extended-back petals were overlapped in Figure 50*b*, and make the rest of the bud like that in Figure 50*l* (Fig. 50*m*).

Make an extended petal rose like the one in Figure 50*g* (Fig. 50*n*.) Overlap three narrow extended-back petals, and then finish it like one in Figure 50*g* (Fig. 50*o*).

Make a rose like the one in Figure 50*o*, but add an extra vertical extended-back petal at the last (Fig. 50*p*).

Drop three S-shaped No. 3 green stems for a corsage arrangement (DC 55, 57 ff.) as at the bottom left of Figure 50. Add three roses at different stages of development. Then add receptacle, the rounded green base out of which sepals and flowers grow, to the base of each rose with a No. 3 green cone and bulb technique (pp. 33 ff.): add two, three, four, or five green sepals to base of each rose, depending upon how many show to good advantage in the arrangement.

A real rose has five sepals. When you are making sepals that go down over the receptacle or down over the receptacle and against the stem, hold the $3/16$-inch V-cone in the same position as for vertical leaves (pp. 45–47). Start the sepal at the point where receptacle and flower join, and then bring the V-cone downward.

Using a ¼-inch and then a ⅜-inch V-cone, add several veined tapered rose leaves of different sizes and at different angles (pp. 43 ff.).

Drop two S-shaped No. 3 green stems for the arrangements at the right side of Figure 50. Form flowers, receptacles, and then sepals on both stems. Form ⅜-inch V-cone leaves on the upper stem in an S-shaped curve to make the arrangement more graceful; and make thorns on the lower stem with a No. 2 green cone and cone star technique (DC 70 ff.).

Draw a No. 2 green stem in a graceful curve to the right. Add ¼-inch V-cone leaves to the small stem and a ⅜-inch V-cone leaf to the left side of main stem.

Use 3-D roses instead of sweet peas in the arrangement in Figure 40. (Use proper greenery.) Roses are white, pink, red, yellow, and intermediate tones. Try using 3-D roses in place of nail roses in the various arrangements in DC 58, 64, 95, 96, 101, 102, and frontispiece and in 27C, 6, 11, 12, and 30.

HALF-TULIPS

Using a No. 5 cone of soft white icing and bulb technique (pp. 33 ff.), form an almond-shaped mound of icing, with the largest part nearest you (Fig. 51a). Turn cake around so that the point of the "almond" is nearest you (use a turntable or Lazy Susan to make turning easier), and make a white No. 125 extended-back petal. (The base of the tube goes along the high center of the "almond"; the top of the tube is tilted downward and held next to the surface. Fig. 51b.)

Turn the cake around so that point of "almond" is away from you and, starting at the bottom center of the flower and going to the right, make a narrow extended-back petal (Fig. 51c).

Now, starting at the bottom center of the flower and going to the left, make a narrow extended-back petal that almost touches or slightly overlaps the left edge of the right petal (Fig. 51*d*).

Point petals slightly between thumb and fingers after they dry for a few minutes, or use corn starch or water on your fingers and point the petals immediately after they are made.

Shape the base of the flower so that it is round and smooth (Fig. 51*e*).

Make "almonds" of different sizes on a cake surface that has been iced a light green. (Make the larger ones in the foreground and leave larger spaces between them.) Turn cake around and on each "almond" make the extended-back petal shown in Figure 51*b* (using smaller No. 104 tube for smaller tulips in background), and turn cake again to original position and form petals shown in Figures 51*c,d.* Point tops of petals slightly and make the base of each tulip round and smooth.

Drop long No. 4 green stems for tulips in foreground, and short No. 3 green stems for tulips in background. Make green vertical leaves (pp. 45 f.) with a 1/8-inch V-cone for flowers in background. Cut the V-cone larger from time to time and make leaves for larger flowers in foreground.

Tulips are white, yellow, pink, red, maroon, purple, intermediate shades, and many combinations. Use different-colored tulips in the same top or side arrangement, and make half-tulips with leaf technique, using rounded taper at bottom and top of each petal. Also make half-tulips with a variation of the metal-surface technique used for full tulips on pp. 203 ff.

Many flowers can be made with two or more techniques. For instance, morning-glories (pp. 22–23) can also be made with the shallow-nail technique used for petunias (pp. 190–92). Lilies of the valley (DC 43 ff.) can be made with bulb technique, star pop-up technique (pp. 13 ff.), or the system that is used for making centers for narcissuses (pp. 163–65). Chrysanthemums, daisies, and zinnias can be formed with leaf tech-

FIGURE 51

nique, U-tube leaf technique (pp. 81–84), or a small flower tube and flat-flower method (pp. 49–52). There are many others that you have probably discovered or will discover as you progress.

Form flowers according to the techniques you prefer. What

works well for one person may not be as effective or as convenient for another. If the completed flowers are attractive, that is all that really matters.

MONKSHOOD

Using a No. 103 white cone, make a high-angled simple back petal (Fig. 52*a*). Then make the same kind of petal but start at the lower left side of the first petal and go halfway to the top center of it (Fig. 52*b*). Third, make the same kind of petal but begin at the top center of the first petal, overlapping or not overlapping the second petal, and bring the third petal to the lower right side of flower (Fig. 52*c*).

Turn surface around so that top of flower is nearest you and make a low-angle, no-tilt extended-center petal from the center of the flower to the left (Fig. 52*d*). Now make a similar petal to the right (Fig. 52*e*).

Put several very small egg-yellow dots in the center of the flower with a fine paper-cone opening (Fig. 52*f*). Turn the surface around so that last two petals of the flowers are nearest you and the flower is right side up.

Using a No. 3 dark-green cone, push the tube into icing as it is being formed to make deeply lobed leaves. (Study pp. 47–49). Drop a stem at the center with the same cone and make three green bulbs of icing at the top of the stem.

Now and then overlapping petals, make monkshood flowers directly on cake. Make each bud near the top of the stem with two low-angled, simple back petals, one on top of the other. (Have the base of the tube away from the stem. Have the top of the tube almost touching the stem.) Add small stems and sepals to the buds.

Monkshood flowers are dark blue, pink, white, or blue and white; the leaves are a dark green.

Many flowers intrigue us with their unusual structure and their unusual and vivid names: monkshood, Dutchman's-

FIGURE 52

breeches, bleeding hearts, Jack-in-the-pulpits, adder's-tongues, butter-and-eggs, arrowheads, sweet Williams, cup-and-saucers, snapdragons, painted tongues, babies'-breath, red hot poker. Lively imaginations of forgotten generations have endowed them with a folklore that will endure as long as flowers and men share the universe.

CHAPTER X

Apple Blossoms and Similar Flat Flowers

APPLE BLOSSOMS

APPLE BLOSSOMS, and many other flowers, are composed princi-
pally of extended-back petals, which may be made in three
different ways: on a platform of icing and a flower nail, on a
metal surface, or on a square of waxed paper and a flower nail.
One or more of these methods are also used for many flowers
other than "flat flowers." You have already made some of the
nonflat flowers with these methods, and you will make others
later. Because of this extensive use the following discussion
of the three methods of making apple blossoms is very important.

The platform method of making apple blossoms is given in
detail in *Decorating Cakes for Fun and Profit,* pp. 46 ff., and
the steps are also illustrated in the first eight parts of Figure 53.
This method has the advantage that the flower can be made
on a nail and then transferred immediately to a cake. (See
pp. 144 f. for triple-tone method of coloring icing for apple
blossoms.) This is accomplished by making a No. 104 two-level
circular platform of icing against a No. 7 flower nail (Figs.
53*a,b*), and then making the flower on top of that. The flower
is removed by inserting a knife between the top of the nail and
the icing platform and turning the nail until platform and
flower are on the knife. Then platform and flower are pushed
from the knife onto the cake with flower nail or another
instrument.

The next eight parts of Figure 53 show the steps for making apple blossoms by the metal-surface technique. (This is the quickest method.)

The metal surface can be one of the metal dividers used to separate ice-cube dividers in wide trays; this is a handy size for a small freezing element. If you have a large deep-freeze compartment in your refrigerator or a large deep-freeze cabinet, you can use a smooth-surfaced cookie sheet or any other convenient pan. The large, flat metal cans of liquid ice or similar products used in picnic baskets are also very useful, especially for the full tulips and iris described in Chapter XIV. Cans of liquid ice and similar products may be bought in hardware, drug, and department stores; after they are frozen thoroughly, they stay very cold for several hours at ordinary room temperatures.

Be sure to wipe frost off the largest surface on which you intend to work, or the frost will melt at room temperature and spoil your flowers by adding moisture to them. Place a towel under the can of liquid ice to keep it from sliding and to soak up moisture formed as the frost on the outside of the can melts.

After you have made buttercream flowers against any metal surface (including liquid-ice cans), place them in a small or large freezing compartment for four minutes or more. Then loosen the frozen flowers from the metal surface with a thin, sharp knife. The metal surface will keep them cold and firm while you place them in an arrangement or while you put them on unglazed cardboard to dry. (Unglazed cardboard acts as a blotter and speeds the drying.)

Once the flowers are removed from the freezing compartment, do not leave them on the cold metal surface longer than necessary; moisture in the air condenses on the cold metal and softens the flowers.

If you intend to put the flowers in an arrangement immedi-

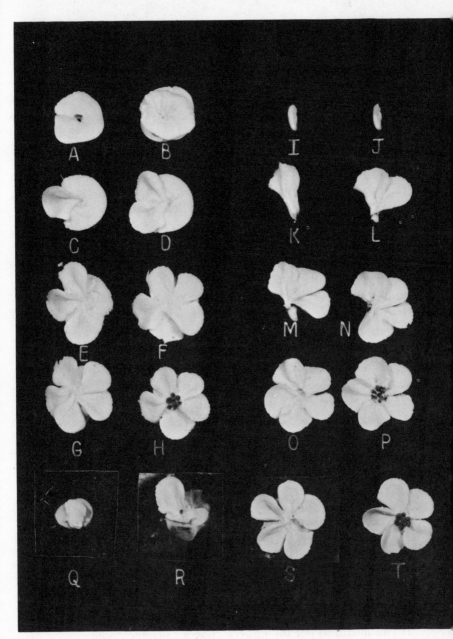

FIGURE 53

ately, leave them in the freezing compartment until the stems and necessary leaves have been formed on the cake. If you intend to dry the flowers a short time or overnight, remove them quickly from the metal surface as soon as you take them out of the freezing compartment and place them on unglazed cardboard.

If a freezing compartment is unavailable, leave the flowers on a shelf in the refrigerator for fifteen to thirty minutes, depending upon the size of the flower and the efficiency of the refrigerator.

When mechanical refrigeration is unavailable, put the metal surface directly on top of ice or dry ice that has been placed in a deep pan. Wait until the flowers are cold enough to hold their shape; then remove them from the metal surface with a sharp knife.

When no refrigeration of any kind is available, make flowers directly on unglazed cardboard. Let them dry overnight (or for several hours, if the air is dry enough) before removing them with a sharp knife and placing them in an arrangement.

The direct platform method described on pp. 136 f. can also be employed when you wish to make and use buttercream flowers of this type immediately without the help of refrigeration. Do not attempt to keep buttercream flowers for more than an hour or so on ordinary refrigerator shelves. When they are left too long and are then brought out into a warm room, they soon become softer than they were when you first made them, because of additional moisture that they absorbed in the refrigerator. An efficient deep-freeze compartment, however, will keep buttercream flowers on metal, cardboard, or cake for an indefinite time because of the fact that they do not absorb moisture when they freeze quickly.

Air-dried flowers, of course, can be kept at room temperatures for several weeks if they are kept free of dust in boxes or cabinets. In the business world, especially, it is very important to make up flowers in advance so that they will be ready for immediate use when there is rush business; deep-freezing and air-drying methods for buttercream flowers meet this need efficiently.

Using a No. 104 cone of icing, triple-toned as in description on pp. 144 f., make several rows of small mounds of icing (Figs. 53*i,j*) on metal surface. (These serve merely to hold the petals together at the centers of the flowers so that they will not break apart when they are removed. Ten or a hundred flowers can be made at one time. Be sure to leave enough space between small mounds of icing for flowers to be formed later.)

Using a very low angle and an extreme right tilt, make a single tapered extended-back petal at each mound of icing. (Fig. 53*k*. Place the base of the tube in the mound of icing, make extended-back petal, and bring the base of the tube back to the original position in the mound of icing. Taper the base of each petal in flowers of this type by gradually increasing pressure at the beginning and gradually decreasing pressure at the end. Taper petals in the same manner when they are being made by the other two methods.)

Turn the metal surface slightly to the left so that all flowers will be in a convenient position for making the next petal. Placing the wedge-shaped metal-tube opening a little lower than the right edge of the previous petal and a little to the right of it, add a second petal to each of the small mounds of icing. (Fig. 53*l*. When the second petal begins to form, it slides almost to the right edge of the first petal or slightly under it. Do not underlap petals very much, and do not underlap all of them.)

Turn the metal surface slightly further to the left just before each succeeding petal is made. This makes it possible for you to stay in one position as you make the different petals on the flowers. Using the same technique, add third petals to all of the flowers (Fig. 53*m*), then fourth petals (Fig. 53*n*); finally add fifth petals to all of them (Fig. 53*o*).

Add several very small yellow-green dots with a paper cone to the center of each apple blossom (Fig. 53*p*). Then spread the dry bristles of small brush by tapping them against a flat surface, and touch the bristle tips very lightly to some liquid brown vegetable color. Then touch the colored tips of the spread bristles to the center of each flower just once and very lightly (Fig. 53*p*); several very small dots of brown color can be added at one time in this way.

Put the metal surface in freezing compartment for several minutes; then remove the frozen flowers and put them in arrangement or on cardboard to dry.

See pp. 199 ff. for details concerning metal-surface technique and general information regarding equipment.

The third method of making apple blossoms and other flat flowers, as well as some nonflat flowers, is that of fastening a piece of waxed paper to a No. 7 nail with a little shortening or icing and making the flower on top of the waxed paper. This is easier than the platform method, but it is slower than either the platform (pp. 136 f.) or the metal-surface technique (pp. 199 ff.). Keep a supply of 1½-inch squares of waxed paper in a box for making these and other flowers with the waxed-paper method.

Put shortening or a little icing on a No. 7 nail held in the left hand. Then push the top of flower nail into a box of waxed-paper squares; lift it out. (Usually a single square of paper will stick to the nail. This is easier than trying to pick up a single square of waxed paper by hand.)

Holding a No. 104 cone of icing in right hand, press the edge of the right hand against the waxed paper to make sure that it is firmly in place against the flower nail; this avoids wasting time in needlessly putting down and picking up the same cone between

FIGURE 54

making separate flowers by this method. Make a small mound of icing on the center of the waxed paper with the No. 104 cone (Fig. 53*q*).

Putting the base of the tube in the mound of icing and holding the tube at a very low angle and an extreme right tilt, turn the nail properly (DC 46) a very short distance while the base of the tube is brought ¼-inch toward the outside of the disc, and then is brought back on the same ¼-inch line to the exact starting point. (Gradually increase and decrease pressure on the icing as the petal is being formed. See illustrations and text, DC 46 ff., for more detailed instructions.)

Make the next four petals in a similar way (Fig. 53*s*). Then place waxed paper and flower on metal surface.

Make several more apple blossoms in the same way and place them with the first one. Make centers as in Figure 53*p*, and put the metal tray of flowers in a freezing compartment for five minutes or more. Finally, remove the waxed papers from the frozen flowers and place the flowers in arrangement immediately or on an unglazed cardboard to dry for later use (Fig. 53*t*).

Make the first third of the main branch with a No. 5 brown cone, using bulb technique with the cone nearly horizontal and gradually decreasing pressure (Fig. 54). Form the next third with a No. 3 brown cone and drop technique, and the last third with the No. 3 brown cone and drawing technique. Form twigs with No. 3 brown cone and drop technique. Then with a No. 2 green cone and drawing technique, make the small bud and flower stems that will show.

Use a ⅜-inch V-cone for leaves. Make buds with No. 3 pink cone and bulb technique, and make No. 3 green sepals around white buds. (Study the three methods of arranging leaves with flowers as described on pp. 58–60.). Place the flowers in the arrangement.

In order to convince you that the three methods described above produce about the same results if they are used properly, the arrangement in Figure 54 is composed in equal numbers of apple blossoms made by all three methods.

Apple blossoms are used in a basket arrangement in *Decorating Cakes for Fun and Profit,* p. 65, and in a corsage arrangement in *27 Special Creations,* p. 3. In many situations apple blossoms made with a No. 103 or smaller flower tube will be more appropriate.

Some apple blossoms are almost white; others, when seen in large clusters, are a light pink, though when examined individually they appear less pink.

Many other flowers, including some roses, are also colored in this delicate and elusive way. To help give this same effect with icing, we suggest that you try what we call "triple-toning" rather than the blending of white and light pink icing described in DC 24 f. The following description is intended for a No. 104 triple-toned cone of icing to be used in making apple blossoms. However, the method of filling a cone can be used for any flower, ribbon, bird, or any other subject that requires subtle shading.

Prepare white icing, very light-pink icing, light-pink icing, and a paper cone.

Working with a small table knife at the left side of a mound of white icing, cut away a very small amount and keep it on the lower side of the knife. Holding the paper cone in the proper position so that the loose inside edge of paper is above the left thumb (illustrated in DC 22 ff.), place point of knife as close as possible to the *inside* point of the cone. Keeping icing on lower side of the knife, press the knife firmly against the paper above the left thumb as the knife is withdrawn. (This will leave a precise amount of icing near the point and on the lower side of the cone.)

Cut away a slightly larger amount of white icing and keep it on the lower side of the knife as you place it just above the icing already in the cone. Then cut away a still larger amount of white icing and place it above the second amount. (This will fill the cone along one side, starting with a thin strip at the bottom, which gradually becomes thicker until it stops at a point one-third of the way from the top.) In a similar way put a wedge-shaped portion of very light pink icing on top of the white icing.

Now turn the cone so that the white and very light pink icing are on top. Fill the empty space in the cone above your left thumb with light pink icing.

Fold the cone at top. Cut the point off the cone so that the last third of the metal tube will be free of paper.

Place the base of No. 104 flower tube opposite the darkest pink icing. Place the cone and the tube carefully inside a second cone and fold the top of cone.

Make a ribbon of icing. If darkest pink icing does not come out of the base of the tube, turn the metal tube and test repeatedly until it does.

You will notice that there is no sharp division of color in flower petals made with the triple-toning method. It becomes impossible to tell where the white starts and the very light pink ends.

FORGET-ME-NOTS

The arrangement of forget-me-nots at the left of Figure 55 is made with a drop-flower tube. There are many such tubes available, and some of them are especially useful for making uniform small flowers quickly. Drop-flower tubes usually produce a flower of five or more petals with one pressure or pressure-and-turn. The center is often added with a plain tube and icing of a different color.

Drop-flower tubes can be used to good advantage when you decorate many small pastries or cookies with a simple, uniform design. You can also use them for borders and drapery in place

FIGURE 55

of star work (DC 78 f.).* In the left half of Figure 55 we used No. 93, one of the forget-me-not tubes, to produce quickly a colorful and interesting arrangement suitable for a rectangular cake. By turning the main stem a little more to the right, you can make it fit a round layer cake.

Use drop technique (DC 53 f.) to make the main stem with a No. 3 cone of soft green icing. Use drawing technique (DC 27 f.) and a No. 3 green cone to make small stems. (Drawing technique reduces the quantity of icing that leaves the tube and therefore reduces the width of the stems.)

Using bulb technique (pp. 33 ff.) and the same cone, make the stems larger where small stems branch away from the main one.

When preparing a cone with soft light-blue icing, be careful to keep the last half of the inside of a No. 93 metal tube free of paper if you are using the double-cone method. Otherwise, the shaft inside the metal tube will bend the inner paper cone and keep the icing from coming out of the tube in a smooth, even fashion.

Wherever flowers are to be placed, hold the No. 93 cone of soft light-blue icing vertically to the surface of the cake. Press the point of metal tube below surface of cake icing. Exert pressure to form a five-petaled flower. Continue in this manner until all the flowers are made.

Add the flower centers with a dot of yellow icing from a No. 2 cone. Then make green leaves with a 1/4-inch V-cone.

Drop the two parts of the main stem in the arrangement to the right (Fig. 55) with a No. 3 green cone, and draw the small stems with the same cone. Using bulb technique and the same cone, enlarge the stems where they come together.

Make green leaves with a 1/4-inch V-cone.

---

* "DC" indicates pages in *Decorating Cakes for Fun and Profit;* "27C," pages in *27 Special Creations for Cake Decorators.*

FIGURE 56

Using a No. 101s flower tube and soft white icing, make very small flowers that look like apple blossoms (pp. 136 ff.) on a metal surface (pp. 199 ff.). Make centers with a single dot of yellow icing from a No. 2 cone.

Freeze flowers for three minutes or more. Then remove them with a sharp, thin knife and place them against little green dots of icing in the arrangement so that they are tilted at different angles. Let a few flowers overlap each other.

Forget-me-nots are blue or white. When used to emphasize a sentimental theme, the blue variety are the only ones considered.

The second method of making forget-me-nots is not as fast as the first one, but it is more realistic. The metal-surface technique, however, speeds up the second method considerably.

Pink or white babies'-breath are smaller than forget-me-nots but very similar.

Using a No. 101 pink cone and metal-surface technique, make a dozen small flowers that look like apple blossoms (Fig. 56. You can also use platform and waxed-paper methods described on pp. 136 ff.). Make the center of each arbutus flower with a small dot of yellow icing made with a No. 2 cone. Then freeze the flowers for four minutes or more.

Do not remove the flowers from freezer until leaves, stems, and buds are made on the cake. Flowers will keep perfectly for an indefinite time as long as they are frozen.

Form a heavy vine with No. 4 paper cone of soft brown icing, holding the cone nearly horizontal to the surface and using bulb technique. Draw small stems with same cone.

Form green leaves with a ⅜-inch V-cone, tapering them very little (study pp. 66–69 for special technique). Brush leaves with liquid brown vegetable color. (Use brown paste color and water, or mix liquid green, yellow, and red vegetable colors to produce brown.)

Overlapping two low-angled, medium-tilted simple center petals (pp. 102 ff.), make the small buds at left with a No. 101 pink cone. Make small sepals at the base of each bud with a No. 2 green cone and leaf pressure technique.

Take the flowers out of the freezer and remove them from the metal surface with a thin, sharp knife. Place the flowers in the arrangement so that several are on top of others.

Trailing-arbutus flowers are pink or white, and in a corsage arrangement they are a natural. Make an irregular vine around the top or bottom edge of a cake. Make clusters of flowers against leaves at intervals and make occasional leaves on small stems between clusters of flowers.

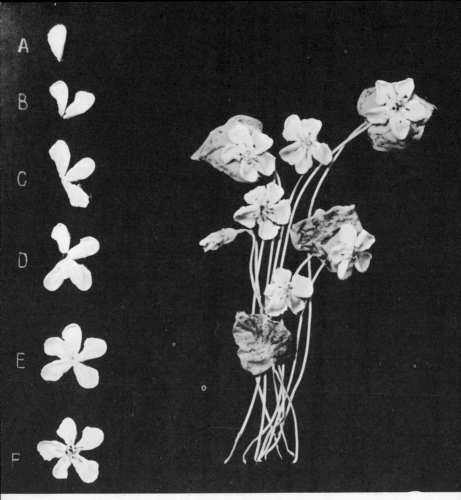

FIGURE 57

VIOLETS

Make several violets with a No. 103 white cone, but separate the narrow petals more frequently and more widely than you did while making apple blossoms (Figs. 57a–e). Make two of the petals a little smaller than the others, and overlap petals occasionally. (Use the waxed-paper method, pp. 136 ff., or the metal-surface method, pp. 199 ff.; the petal arrangement is too open and exposes the platform if the platform method is used.)

Put several fine light-yellow-green dots of icing in the center of each flower with a small paper cone (Fig. 57*f*). Touch the center of each flower lightly with a dry, open brush and red vegetable color. (See p. 141 for the method for adding brown color to the centers of apple blossoms.)

Streak petals lightly along the center with a brush and light-pink vegetable color. (Blue or purple violets are streaked with yellow.)

Freeze the violets for four or five minutes.

Drop graceful double-curved No. 2 green stems for leaves and flowers. Make green leaves with ½-inch V-cone, using the technique shown on pp. 66–69 to add icing and make the leaves heart-shaped. Then brush brown color on the leaves, if you wish.

To form the bud at the left, put two or three No. 103 low-angled, simple center petals at end of stem. Make sepals as for sweet peas (pp. 120–26) at the base of the bud with a No. 2 green cone.

Remove the frozen violets from the waxed paper or the metal surface and place them on little green dots at the ends of the flower stems. Tilt them at various angles.

When the flowers begin to thaw, shape a petal here and there a little differently so that no two violets will look the same.

This variety of violets is white, purple, blue, and yellow. There are many other types of violets and violet leaves. Many African violets, for instance, have tapered leaves and tapered petals. Those in Figure 57 are one of the old-fashioned varieties.

Make a thick bouquet of violets by putting a small piece of cake on top of a layer cake. Cover the small piece with light-green icing, and make two dozen violets with metal-surface technique and freeze them.

Drop many No. 2 curved green stems from the center of the arrangement to points about three inches below the center. Make several leaves where the edge of the small piece of cake meets the surface of the layer cake, but omit leaves in the stem area. Remove frozen violets from metal surface and put them on top of and around the sides of the small green-iced piece of cake so that they overlap each other and parts of the leaves.

Study real flowers, seed catalogues, and books about flowers. You will notice that violet technique can be adapted to making begonias. Notice petal structure and the unusual center, and study the unique stem and leaf structure. Brush lukewarm, clear piping jelly on flowers to give them a waxy appearance, and on leaves to make them look glossy. Show begonias in a plant jar or window box.

"Varnish" the butter-yellow petals of buttercups with lukewarm clear piping jelly. See illustration on p. 57. Mix some clear piping jelly with buttercream icing when you wish to give leaves and flower petals a glossy appearance; holly leaves and poinsettias are especially beautiful when this mixture is used.

With modifications, the apple-blossom technique can also be used for orange blossoms, cherry blossoms, sweet Williams, verbena, Japanese windflower, geraniums, heliotrope, phlox, and many similar ones.

Still other varieties of flat flowers are described in the next chapter.

CHAPTER XI

Other Varieties of Flat Flowers

THE FLOWERS in this chapter can be made by any of the three basic methods used for apple blossoms (pp. 136 ff.): platform, waxed-paper, or metal-surface. They differ widely from the latter in the method of their construction.

COTTAGE PINKS

Make a narrow, ridged extended-back petal (pp. 115 f.) with a No. 103 white cone on a metal surface (Fig. 58*a*; see pinks in color in frontispiece). Add three more narrow, ridged extended-back petals to the first one (Figs. 58*b–d*). Finally, add the fifth narrow, ridged extended-back petal to the first four (Fig. 58*e*) but overlap petals very little.

Brush some pink coloring on the center. With a very fine paper cone make several small upright threads of yellow icing at the center.

Make several more flowers on the metal surface and freeze them.

Drop curved No. 2 green stems for buds and flowers. (Notice that there is only one flower or bud to a stem.) Make narrow vertical leaves (p. 47) with a ¼-inch V-cone and bluish-green icing.

Using a No. 3 green cone and bulb technique, form a cone-shaped mound of green icing (as for carnations, pp. 175 f.) at the top of each flower stem. And at the top of each mound form a ball of green icing so that flowers can be tilted to various natural angles when they are later placed on stems.

Make the buds at top left with a No. 3 green cone and bulb technique.

Remove the frozen flowers from the metal surface with a sharp knife and place them at the tops of stems. If some petals droop too much when they start to thaw, brace them in position with a little green icing.

The best method is to air-dry the pinks on cardboard overnight and put them on the stems the next day. Then the petals will not droop when the flowers are placed at extreme angles. The ones in Figure 58 were handled in this manner. Part of them are pink and part are white.

Cottage pinks are white, pink, red, lavender, or variegated. They are related to carnations, which we will study in the next chapter.

BLANKETFLOWERS

Use the waxed-paper method for making blanketflowers, also called Gaillardias. (Fig. 59). The metal-surface method can be used, but it is a little awkward in this case.

Fasten a square of waxed paper to a No. 7 nail with shortening or icing. Place the base of a No. 103 yellow cone at the center of the waxed paper and hold the metal tube at a low angle and an extreme right tilt. As you press the icing, move the tube ¼-inch from the center toward the outside edge of nail and back to center. (Do not turn nail.) Repeat this movement three or four times (Fig. 59*a*); then stop pressure.

Turn the nail slightly so that it is in position for the next petal. Watching spacing carefully, make seven more petals like the first one. (Fig. 59*b*. Turn nail between petals, *not* while they are being formed.)

Make a ball of yellow icing in the center of the flower with a No. 5 cone and bulb technique (Fig. 59*c*). Turn the nail upside down and dip the top of the center into gold Glamor-Glitter or

FIGURE 58

into coarse granulated sugar that has been colored yellow. Then, using red color, touch a brush at several points around the top edge of the center (Fig. 59*c*). Or you can leave the whole flower a plain yellow, or brush brown-orange color near the center of the flower (Fig. 59*c*).

Remove the waxed-paper and the flower from the nail and freeze them for five minutes or more.

Drop a No. 4 green stem; draw a small stem with the same cone.

Make a ball of yellow icing at the end of the small stem with a No. 5 cone and bulb technique. Brush the yellow bud with brown-orange color so that it is spotted. Then, using a 1/16-inch V-cone, make many small sepals that point downward from the bottom edge of the bud.

Make two leaves with 3/8-inch V-cone and back-away leaf technique (p. 52). Smooth them with a moist brush or finger, or let them dry and touch them lightly when they are no longer sticky.

Put a ball of green icing at top of main stem. Remove frozen flower from paper and tilt it against the ball of icing.

More brown-orange color was applied to the flower in the arrangement in order to show another variation. Gaillardias, or blanketflowers, are golden, ruby red, or bronze and yellow. Coreopsis and cosmos can be made in a similar way.

PANSIES

Make pansies by any of the three methods used for apple blossoms. You can also form them directly against the cake itself, but you can tilt them more naturally when you make them separately and then place them on the cake.

Using a No. 104 blue cone, make a wavy extended-back petal (Fig. 60*a*).

FIGURE 59

The white edge to the petal was added for the sake of photographic clarity. Sometimes we variegated white and blue icing in the same cone in order to achieve a similar result (Fig. 60*e*). We brushed blue color on the edges of white petals for the same reason. Actually, the result resembles some of the unusual combinations found in real pansies.

Make a second wavy extended-back petal that overlaps the first one and goes to the right of it (Fig. 60*b*). Make a white narrow, wavy extended-back petal that goes a little to the left of the first petal and overlaps both the first and second petals. (Fig. 60*c*. Notice that all petals start with the base of the tube at the same point, which becomes the center of the pansy.)

Repeat Figure 60*c*, but this time bring the petal to the right (Fig. 60*d*). Make a very wide white extended-back petal with a slight dip at the center of the outside edge. (Fig. 60*e*. Place this petal so that it does not extend to the left or right as far as the

157

third and fourth petals do, but so that it does overlap the lower parts of the third and fourth petals.)

Make a small No. 3 flat dot of yellow icing at the center, and make two small No. 3 flat dots of white icing just above the yellow one.

Using a fine brush and blue vegetable color, paint the three lower petals. (Fig. 60e. Make streaks of color very fine as they approach outer edges of petals.)

Drop one No. 3 green stem for each flower and bud. Using a ⅜-inch V-cone, make tapered, heavily veined leaves so that the edges are rough (p. 52). Make a ball of green icing at the top of each stem, and tilt a flower against each ball of green icing.

Make the bud with a No. 3 white cone and a No. 3 green cone. Brush white icing with blue color to represent the unopened flower.

Add a few leaves so that they overlap edges of some flowers. If you wish, touch the leaves with a brush and brown color.

Pansies are white, yellow, lavender, blue, purple, red, and various combinations. We have indicated a few of the possible variations in the arrangement in Figure 60.

DOGWOOD

Dogwood flowers can be made directly against the cake surface; but they can be tilted more naturally if they are made separately by a technique that you prefer before they are placed in an arrangement (Fig. 61 and frontispiece).

Using a No. 104 white cone at a medium angle and an extreme right tilt, form a wide, slightly cupped extended-back petal (Fig. 61a). Placing the base of the tube at the previous starting point, form a similar petal opposite to the first one (Fig. 61b). Then, placing the base of the tube at the previous starting point, form a narrow, tapered, slightly cupped extended-back petal to the right so that it just barely overlaps the large petals, or does not

FIGURE 60

overlap them at all (Fig. 61*c*). Placing the base of the tube at the previous starting point, form a second petal like the one in Figure 61*c,* but bring it to the left (Fig. 61*d*). Push a moist brush handle or similar tool into the center of the outside edge of each petal, and turn the handle between your fingers to form a rounded notch. (Fig. 61*e*. Dip brush handle in water frequently.) Brush the edge of each notch with pink vegetable color (Fig. 61*f*).

Form a large, thick mound of light-yellow-green No. 2 dots at the flower center (Fig. 61*g*); add very fine dots of brown color to center, using method for apple blossoms (Fig. 61*h*; see also p. 141).

Drop No. 4 brown main branches with a paper-cone opening. Drop No. 2 brown small twigs with a paper-cone opening. (Notice that each flower has its own twig and that branches are forked at the ends.)

Using a 3/16-inch V-cone of light-green icing, make two well-tapered leaves opposite each other and at the base of each twig that bears a flower. Then put a small mound of brown icing at the top of each flower-bearing twig, and tilt the dogwood flowers made with a No. 102 tube against the mounds of brown icing.

The flowers made with a No. 104 tube are more nearly life-size; those made with a No. 102 tube are miniatures. By using a No. 101*s* tube, you can make them small enough for sugar cubes or mints. Use royal icing (DC, p. 124) or fondant icing (which can be made or bought) when you wish to decorate sugar cubes, mints, chocolates, or other candy.

Dogwood flowers are white with pink at the edge of each petal, or pink variegated with white toward the center and brown at the edge of each petal. Dogwood is used in a wreath design, 27C 5.

Just a reminder: When extended-back petals or simple back petals are being formed with the aid of a flower nail, turn the

FIGURE 61

nail slightly. Do *not* turn wrist or arm, which are turned only when making back petals directly against a metal, cake, or other surface that is not being turned.

The flowers in the next chapter are more complex but no more difficult than those you have already learned.

FIGURE 62

CHAPTER XII

Complex Nail Flowers

WITH THE EXCEPTION of the half-carnation, the flowers in this chapter are usually made with waxed paper and a No. 7 nail. The platform and metal-surface techniques are sometimes used for narcissuses and daffodils.

Dahlias, water lilies, peonies, and full carnations are made more conveniently with waxed paper and flower nail because they must be turned a great deal while they are being made. The other methods can be used for these also.

NARCISSUS

Using a white No. 104 cone, make a small spot of icing at the center of a square of waxed paper previously fastened to a No. 7 nail. Make three narrow, tapered extended-back petals in the shape of a triangle (Figs. 62a–c).

Remember to turn the nail very little or not at all while a petal is being formed. The base of the tube moves out toward the edge of the nail and back to center along a ¼-inch line. Do not turn your wrist or arm.

Make three more narrow, tapered extended-back petals on top of and slightly overlapping the edges of the first three petals (Figs. 62d–f).

Make a spot of soft yellow icing with a No. 3 tube (Fig. 62g, first part). Holding the No. 3 cone of soft yellow icing almost vertically and pressing the tube lightly against the spot of icing, spiral upward ⅜-inch off the surface, making each succeeding circle slightly larger than the preceding one. (Fig. 62g, second part. Figure 62*g*, third part, shows the conelike center as it would appear if it were tilted to one side.)

After the petals of narcissus have dried a few minutes and are no longer sticky, point them between thumb and finger. (If you are in a hurry, use corn starch or water on your fingers and then point petals: Fig. 62*h*).

Remove the waxed paper and the flower from the nail and place them on a metal surface. Make a spot of yellow icing in the center of the narcissus (Fig. 62*h*), and form a yellow spiral center as shown in Figure 62*g*.

Put a No. 2 dot of orange icing in the bottom of the yellow cone (Fig. 62*i*). Using a fine brush and red vegetable color, lightly touch top *outside* edge of the yellow cone at many different points (Fig. 62*j*).

Make several narcissuses and freeze them for four or five minutes. Then remove them from the papers and place them on unglazed cardboard to dry. Place them on the cake at the last possible moment so that they will be drier and firmer and hold their shape better. (If possible, let them dry overnight.)

Using a 3/16-inch V-cone of green icing and vertical leaf technique (pp. 45–47), make two large leaves of different length. Make four No. 3 green stems in number-7 style.

The narcissus and violet families as well as many others have stems that are shaped like 7. Notice the stem for the flower at the right and the stem for the bud in Figure 62. This style looks something like a hockey stick upside down.

Make a tannish husk at the top part of each stem with a No. 3 cone, and a short vertical leaf in the center on top of the stems. Make the bud directly against the cake with a No. 104 white cone and a series of low-angled simple center petals.

Make a mound of soft green icing at the top of each stem with No. 3 cone and bulb technique. Remove the dried flowers from the unglazed cardboard and tilt them at different angles against the mounds of soft green icing. If the flowers are not firm enough to hold their shape, brace them by putting a little green icing underneath weak petals.

There are many kinds of narcissuses. The petals may be rounded or pointed, white or yellow. The centers may be orange or yellow, small and low or large and high. The centers in Figure 62 can also be made with a No. 103 yellow cone by holding the base of the tube at the center and tilting the top of the tube to the right while the nail is being turned and the icing is being pressed.

DAFFODILS

Using a No. 125 light-yellow cone and a No. 7 nail with waxed paper, make a small mound of icing on the center of the waxed paper. Using the same cone, make three narrow, tapered extended-back petals in the shape of a triangle (Fig. 63*a*). Make three more narrow, tapered extended-back petals on top of and slightly overlapping the edges of the first three petals (Fig. 63*b*). Point petals between thumb and finger (Fig. 63*c*).

Placing the base of No. 125 *dark*-yellow cone at the center of daffodil and tilting the top of the tube slightly to the right, turn the nail while exerting pressure to form a trumpet center (Fig. 63*d*).

Add six No. 2 yellow dots of icing in a circle in the bottom of the trumpet to represent stamens. Using cone star technique and a No. 2 yellow cone, make a high pistil in the center of the dots (Fig. 63*d*).

Placing the base of a No. 101*s* dark yellow cone at the top edge of the trumpet, tilt the top of the tube to the right and form the fringe at the top edge of trumpet by moving the tube up and down in a diagonal way while turning nail and exerting pressure on the icing (Fig. 63*e*).

Make several daffodils and freeze them for eight or ten minutes.

Remove the frozen flowers from the papers and place them on unglazed cardboard to dry, preferably overnight.

Using a ⅜-inch V-cone of green icing and vertical-leaf technique (pp. 45–47), make three large leaves of different length and shape. Then make three No. 4 green stems in number-7 style (p. 82), and add tannish husk at the top part of each stem with a No. 3 cone.

Form a mound of soft green icing at the top of each stem with a No. 4 cone and bulb technique. Remove the dried flowers from the unglazed cardboard and tilt them at different angles against the mounds of soft green icing. If the daffodils are not firm enough to hold their shape, brace them by putting a little green icing underneath weak petals.

Jonquils are very similar but usually smaller, though some small varieties of daffodils are no larger than some large varieties of jonquils. Daffodils are yellow, white, and pink. The center sometimes contrasts with the petals. One example is a white daffodil with a yellow trumpet.

DAHLIAS

Using a No. 104 white cone and a low angle with an extreme right tilt, make ten narrow extended-back petals on top of waxed paper and a No. 7 nail. (Fig. 64*a*. Turn nail *after* each petal is made—do not turn it *while* the petal is being formed.) Bring each petal to a point between thumb and finger. (Fig. 64*b*. It may be necessary to dip fingers in water or corn starch now and then to keep them from becoming sticky.)

Using a No. 104 white cone and a high angle, with a medium right tilt, make ten short, narrow extended-back petals on top of the first layer of petals. Bring each of them to a point (Fig. 64*c*).

Using a No. 80 white cone and leaf technique at a 45-degree angle, make eight short petals on top of the second layer (Fig. 64*d*). Then, using the same cone and leaf technique but at an 80-degree angle, make eight very short petals on top of the third layer of petals (Fig. 64*e*).

Remove the waxed paper and the dahlia from the nail and

Figure 63

place them on a metal surface. Make several other flowers and freeze them for ten minutes or more.

Drop three No. 3 long green stems; then draw two No. 3 short green stems so that they come out of the long ones.

Using a ⅜-inch V-cone, and later cutting it to a ½-inch V-cone, make green well-tapered leaves, after studying variety of leaf formation on pp. 41 ff. Then add buds by using bulb technique and a No. 3 green cone. Using a ⅛-inch V-cone of green icing, make sepals at the base of each bud. With a No. 3 cone, add a white fringe to the bud at the right.

Make a mound of green icing at the top of each of the three long stems; remove three frozen flowers from the waxed paper and place them at different angles against the mounds of icing.

Dahlias and the remaining flowers in this chapter do not need air-drying, because their heavier construction keeps them from collapsing. Of course, they and all other buttercream flowers can be made up, dried, and stored for later use.

Dahlias are white, yellow, pink, red, maroon, purple, and intermediate shades. Some "pom" varieties are very small. You can use leaf technique with a No. 81 U-shaped tube and make the petals on the surface of a ball of icing. The small chrysanthemums on pp. 82–84 were made in this way.

Some varieties are very large. They look better in icing when they are done in miniature, as in Figure 64.

WATER LILIES

Using a No. 104 white cone and a low angle with an extreme right tilt, make eight narrow extended-back petals on top of waxed paper and a No. 7 nail (Fig. 65a, and frontispiece); move the base of the tube so that the end of each petal goes beyond edge of nail disc. (Turn nail *after* each petal is made.) Point and cup ends of petals between thumb and finger (Fig. 65b).

168

FIGURE 64

FIGURE 65

Using the same cone at a medium angle and a medium right tilt, make eight shorter, narrower extended-back petals on top of the first layer. Point and cup the tip of each petal (Fig. 65c).

Using the same cone at a high angle and a slight right tilt, make six shorter, narrower extended-back petals on top of the second layer, and point and cup them (Fig. 65*d*).

Make a yellow dot in the center of the water lily with a No. 3 cone. (See lilies in arrangement to right in Fig. 65.) Add two or three circles of very fine yellow dots around the yellow center, or make one circle of small yellow No. 13 stars (see arrangement, Fig. 65).

Make three lilies and freeze them for five minutes or more.

Using a No. 125 cone of medium-green icing, make water-lily leaves with the technique described on pp. 45 f., making those in the background smaller to give illusion of distance.

To make the bud at upper right, use a No. 104 white cone and a No. 7 nail to form a cone of icing as for nail rose (DC 49).*

Make eight or more short center petals that start from the base of the icing cone, as for nail rose (DC 50), and point the tips of the petals with thumb and finger. Trim the base of the bud with a knife, and remove the bud from the nail with a knife and place it in arrangement. Add green sepals to the base of the bud with a 1/8-inch V-cone.

Remove the frozen water lilies from the papers and place them in horizontal position against the cake and parts of leaves.

Pink lotus flowers can be made in a similar fashion. Ice the top of a cake with light blue or blue-green icing. Make arrangement of green lily pads and water lilies. Put inscriptions, if any, on the side of the cake. Figure-pipe a small frog on one of the lily pads with a No. 3 green cone. (Study the technique of figure-piping in DC 83 ff.) The use of birds, animals, and other figure-piping will add interest to your work.

Use the sugar-mold method for making many objects and creatures that will fit in well with the flowers and the arrangements you are learning to make. (Study sugar work in DC

---

* "DC" indicates pages in *Decorating Cakes for Fun and Profit;* "27C," pages in *27 Special Creations for Cake Decorators.*

FIGURE 66

89 ff.) Many sugar objects can be used on the decorated base-board of the cake, as well as on the top. (Notice the dogs, 27C 14, 26, and the rabbits and birds, 27C 24.)

Cookie-cutters can serve as sugar molds for watering cans, pumpkins, flowers, trees, angels, nursery-rhyme and storybook characters, cowboys and Indians, horses, other animals, stars, Christmas stockings, Christmas candles, and countless other subjects. Patronize the kitchenware, toy, and baby counters in department stores. Many toys, including rattles, can be split down the middle and used as molds. And do not fail to notice all the new molds available in bakery-supply and mail-order houses.

PEONIES

Using a No. 104 white cone and a low angle with an extreme right tilt, make eight extended-back petals on waxed paper on a No. 7 nail. (Fig. 66*a* and frontispiece. Turn nail *after* each petal is made.) Then, using the same cone and a medium angle with an extreme right tilt, make eight short extended-back petals on top of first layer of petals (Fig. 66*b*).

Using the same cone and a high angle with a medium tilt, make eight short, narrow extended-back petals on top of the second layer. (Fig. 66*c*). Then point the cone straight down and, placing the base of the tube against third layer of petals, bring the cone straight up as pressure is exerted and then gradually released. Make sixteen of these short, upright petals, some on top of others (Fig. 66*d*).

Make three more peonies and freeze them for five or ten minutes, or longer.

Make a large ball of icing with a No. 5 cone and bulb technique (Fig. 66*e*). Remove the frozen peony from the wax paper and place it on the ball of icing. When the flower begins to thaw and soften, gently bend the first layer of petals downward at various angles (Fig. 66*f*).

FIGURE 67

Drop three long No. 3 green stems. Make a large ball of green icing at the top of each stem with a No. 5 cone and bulb technique.

Make large, well-tapered, heavily ridged leaves (p. 52) with a ½-inch V-cone of green icing. (See below for alternate leaf.)

Remove the frozen peonies from the wax papers and place them at different angles against the balls of green icing at the

174

tops of stems. When the flowers begin to thaw and soften, gently bend the first layer of petals downward at various angles.

If you wish to represent a peony that is not completely open, just push the two bottom layers of petals upward against the rest of the flower as soon as the petals have thawed sufficiently.

Peonies are white, pink, red, maroon, or variegated. Another variety of peonies has complicated divided leaves that you may wish to substitute for the simpler type shown in Figure 66. The divided peony leaves are shown on p. 49.

FULL CARNATIONS

Using a No. 104 cone of stiff white icing and a low angle with an extreme right tilt, make an extended-back petal on waxed paper on a No. 7 nail. Turn the nail as the tube is moved $1/4$-inch away from the center and back. At the same time, make six or seven chopping motions with the tube to make a rough, irregular petal (Fig. 67*a*).

Form five more petals like the first one (Fig. 67*b*).

Make six shorter petals like the first one, overlapping the spaces in the first layer of petals and making only five chopping motions for each petal (Fig. 67*c*). Then form six very short simple back petals, overlapping the spaces in the second layer of petals and making only four chopping motions for each petal (Fig. 67*d*).

Point the cone straight down and, placing the base of the tube against the center of the third layer of petals, bring it straight up as pressure is exerted and then gradually released. Make six of these very small petals in the center (Fig. 67*e*).

Make three carnations and freeze them for five minutes or more.

Drop three long No. 3 medium-green stems. Using a No. 3 medium-green cone and leaf-pressure technique (DC 29, 39 ff.)

or a ⅛-inch V-cone of medium-green icing, make narrow, irregular twin leaves at intervals along the stems.

Bulb a large, elongated mound of icing with a No. 5 light-yellow-green cone at the top of each stem (Fig. 67*f*), making the upper part of the mound twice as high as the lower part so that it will support the carnation at a natural angle. Then, using a No. 3 cone of medium-green icing, with leaf pressure technique make two or more very small leaves at the base of the mound.

Remove the frozen carnations from the waxed papers and place them at appropriate angles against the mounds of icing.

Carnations are white, pink, red, and variegated. White variegated with pink or red is a very pleasing combination. Brush a fine stripe of soft red paste color along the inside of a paper cone from bottom to top. Make the stripe slightly heavier toward the top of the cone. Then put pink or white icing on the opposite side of the cone. Turn the metal flower tube so that a fine line of red-colored icing comes out of the top edge of the tube. The resulting petals are startling and beautiful.

Edges of petals can be made more ragged by using stiff icing and by pinching the top edge of the tube so that the icing breaks slightly when petals are being formed. Flower petals can also be clipped here and there with scissors when they are dry.

Use ferns (pp. 69 f.) and other greenery to show off carnations to best advantage.

HALF-CARNATIONS

The half-carnation is made directly on the cake by a technique that is all its own. It is given in this chapter because, as far as coloring and greenery are concerned, it is the same as the full carnation. However, it is not made like any other buttercream flower. The half-carnation is very effective, nevertheless, and can be made very quickly. It can be used for a complete arrangement, or it can be combined with full carnations.

Note that Figure 68*a* shows the directions in which the No. 104 white cone is moved while each petal is formed. It starts at the *top* and moves from left, to right, to left, to right again. Figure 68*b* shows eight points at which the base of tube chops downward as the cone moves from left, to right, to left, to right again while each petal is being formed.

Using the directions described above and Figures 68*a,b* as a guide and holding a No. 104 white cone at a 45-degree angle, practice making the special half-carnation petal (Fig. 68*c*). Still holding the tube at a 45-degree angle, make two petals that are angled away from each other as though they were at the top of an imaginary V (Fig. 68*d*). Turn the surface so that the point of imaginary V in Figure 68*d* is away from you (Fig. 68*e*).

In other words, the first two petals of each half-carnation have to be made while you are standing, figuratively, beyond the top edge of the illustration and pointing your tube toward the bottom of the illustration.

From this position, make the first two petals for each flower in Figures 68*f–k*. Now turn the surface back again to its original position.

In other words, you are now standing, figuratively speaking, below the lower edge of the illustration and pointing your tube toward the top. All the petals are pointing downward toward you and the lower edge of the illustration.

Using a 45-degree angle and pointing the tube toward the top of the illustration, make the third petal in Figure 68*f* between and slightly above the tops of the first two petals.

Using a high angle for the rest of the flower, place the fourth petal between the left and the center petals so that the top of the flower is rounded (Fig. 68g).

From the fourth petal on, chop the tube downward to the surface of the previous petal but *not* down to the surface of the cake:

Place the fifth petal between the center and the right petals so that the top of the flower is rounded (Fig. 68h). Using a very high angle, place the sixth petal on top of previous petals at the center, but leave a hollow space at the base of flower (Fig. 68j)—do not bring the sixth petal toward you too much, or the flower will be straight at the base.

Bulb a large cylindrical mound of icing at the base of the flower with a No. 5 light yellow-green cone (Fig. 68k), tapering the mound slightly at the bottom.

Holding a No. 104 white cone at an extremely high angle and touching the base of the tube near the top of the green mound, make a wavy, fan-shaped seventh petal that looks something like a large basic extended-back petal (Fig. 68l) made in a vertical position at the back of a 3-D rose (pp. 126 ff.). Make certain that this seventh petal hides the line where the green mound of icing joins the flower.

Drop three long No. 3 medium green stems. (This is an irregular arrangement, in contrast to the one for full carnations in Figure 67.)

Make the bud with two low-angle special half-carnation petals. Form rounded sepals at the base of the bud with same No. 5 cone used for making the cylindrical mound of light yellow-green icing below the bud.

Allowing space enough between tops of stems and first petals of flowers, make two half-carnations. Bring the cylindrical base of each carnation to its stem.

Add very small leaves at the point where the cylindrical base of a carnation joins the stem, as described for full carnation

FIGURE 68

(pp. 175 f.). Add the remainder of leaves to the stems, as described for full-carnation arrangement.

See remarks about the full carnation, above, for a discussion of coloring and related information.

179

CHAPTER XIII

Shallow-Nail Flowers

THE FLOWERS in this chapter, with the exception of the half-nasturtium, are made with a No. 8 shallow nail. The hollow part of the nail is brushed with a thin coat of shortening; then some waxed paper is pressed firmly against the shortening so that the paper stays neatly inside the hollow part of the nail until the flower is completed.

For some flowers, like the Christmas rose and the hibiscus, a simple 2-inch square of waxed paper is satisfactory. If a square piece of waxed paper is used for certain flowers, it has to be slashed at the corners, as shown for the gladiolus (p. 188), in order to fit close enough to the hollow part of the nail.

A waxed-paper cone like the one used for Easter lilies (p. 88) can be used for all deep- and shallow-nail flowers and is recommended if you have any trouble removing well-frozen flowers from square papers. It takes longer to make waxed-paper cones, but they can be saved and reused many times.

Triple-tone the colored icing in the No. 104 cone used for wild roses so that the flower is pink at the center, then light pink, and finally white at the outer edge. Study pp. 144 f. for triple-toning technique, which is used wherever delicate shading is desired.

WILD ROSES

Practice five extended-back petals on a flat surface with a No. 104 triple-toned cone of pink and white icing. Make a slight dip at the center of each petal by moving the tube ⅛-inch toward the center and back again halfway through each petal (Figs. 69 *a–e*).

Make another five-petaled flower in a cone of waxed paper that is fastened to a No. 8 shallow nail with shortening. (Fig. 69*f*. Icing can be used instead of shortening for fastening waxed paper to nail, but it dries out sooner.)

Remove the waxed-paper cone and the flower from the nail and place them on a metal surface. Make several more flowers in waxed-paper cones, put them beside the first one, and freeze the metal tray of flowers for five minutes or more.

Remove one frozen flower from the tray and put the rest of them back into the freezer. Remove the waxed-paper cone from the flower and place the flower upright in a small mound of soft icing. Put a light-yellow-green center in the flower with a No. 3 cone of soft icing (Fig. 69*g*); push a bunch of artificial yellow stamens into the light-yellow-green center and spread the stamens open at the top (Fig. 69*h*).

If the petals of this first flower stay up after they are thawed, make stems and leaves for the arrangement, remove the papers from the other frozen flowers, place them on small mounds of soft green icing at the tops of the stems, and finish them as in Figures 69*g,h*.

But if petals of the first flower do *not* stay up after they are thawed, take the rest of the flowers out of the freezer and air-dry them overnight. Then freeze them for five minutes or more, make stems and leaves for the arrangement, remove the papers from the frozen flowers, place them on small mounds of soft green icing at the tops of the stems, and finish them as in Figures 69*g,h*.

Drop No. 3 green main stems and draw No. 2 small stems out from the main ones.

Using a ¼-inch V-cone of green icing, add five small finely veined rose leaves (p. 131) to each small leaf stem. Using a

⅜-inch V-cone of green icing, add larger finely veined rose leaves that come out singly from the large stems.

Make the small bud at the left with two No. 104 low-angled, overlapped simple center petals (pp. 102 ff.). Add receptacle and sepals to rosebuds as for 3-D roses (pp. 126 ff).

Touch up large stems and all leaves with brush and light-brown vegetable color. Add a small mound of soft green icing at the top of each stem with a No. 3 cone. Then add the frozen wild roses to the mounds of soft green icing and finish them as described in Figures 69*g,h*.

Wild roses are dark pink, light pink, yellow-white, and variegated. The single variety is pictured in Figure 69. You will find that the double variety is easy to make.

Artificial stamens for wild roses, poppies, lilies, etc., can be purchased at bakery-supply houses, mail-order houses, and department stores. Flowers with artificial stamens should be looked at but not eaten. Remove them from a decorated cake before cutting and serving it. Many people like to take them home for souvenirs.

If you wish to be able to eat the flowers, make yellow stamens with a fine paper cone of yellow icing and cone star technique. They will not be as attractive as the artificial ones, but they will be edible.

CHRISTMAS ROSES

Using a No. 125 white cone and a No. 8 shallow nail with waxed paper, form an extended-back petal (Fig. 70*a*). Then complete a flower of five extended-back petals. Point and cup each petal slightly between finger and thumb (Fig. 70*b*).

Make eight Christmas roses and freeze them for ten minutes or more, or air-dry them overnight and then freeze them for ten minutes or more.

They can be made, frozen ten minutes, and used at once,

FIGURE 69

but they must be braced with extra white icing when they are placed in the arrangement; otherwise, some of the petals will droop. If they are air-dried overnight before they are frozen, they need very little, if any, bracing.

Remove the waxed paper from one of the flowers after it is frozen, or dried and frozen. Add a circle of green icing at the center with a No. 4 cone (Fig. 70*c*). Then, using a No. 3 cone, fill the center of the circle with soft yellow icing. Bring fine No. 2 yellow stamens from the yellow center, upward and outward, so that they are above the green circle of icing (Fig. 70*d*).

Drop No. 3 green stems for flowers and leaves. Draw some short stems out of main ones for buds and flowers. (Stems for leaves are more or less horizontal and in the lower part of the arrangement.)

Using a ⅜-inch V-cone of green icing, add tapered and ridged leaves (pp. 52 f.) to the leaf stems only; and brush parts of green leaves with light-brown vegetable color.

Using No. 3 white cone and bulb technique, make carrot-shaped buds at ends of small stems. Then using bulb technique and a No. 3 green cone, form a receptacle for each bud.

Make a mound of soft green icing at the top of each flower stem with a No. 3 cone.

If the flowers have been frozen for ten minutes or more but have not been previously dried for several hours or overnight, remove the papers from them and place the frozen flowers immediately at the tops of the stems. When the petals thaw, brace the weak ones with a little white icing. Finish the centers as in Figures 70*c,d,* after the flowers are on the stems.

If flowers have been dried first and then frozen, remove the papers, place the frozen flowers at the tops of the stems, and finish the centers. (*Very little* bracing, if any, will be required.)

Christmas roses are winter-flowering, and are white or white tinged with pink.

HIBISCUS

Using a No. 125 light-pink cone and No. 8 shallow nail with waxed paper, form a ridged extended-back petal (Fig. 71*a*; see

FIGURE 70

pp. 115 f.) by moving the base of the tube from the center of the nail upward and outward ⅜-inch and then back down to the original starting point while the petal is being formed.

Make the second petal so that it overlaps the first one by one-

FIGURE 71

third or one-fourth of the petal's width (Fig. 71*b*). Make three more petals in a similar manner.

Put fifteen or twenty very small dots of yellow icing in the center (Fig. 71*c*). Make two more hibiscus and freeze them, or dry and then freeze them.

Drop three long No. 4 green stems, and draw short No. 3 green stems out of main ones for buds and leaves.

Using a ½-inch V-cone of green and brown icing (pp. 54–59), make large tapered leaves at the ends of small leaf stems. Now, using a No. 3 cone of soft green icing and bulb technique, form buds on the small stems. Using a No. 2 green cone, make several sepals flare out from the base of each bud.

Add a ball of soft green icing at the top of each long stem with a No. 3 cone; remove the frozen flowers from the papers and place them in tilted position at the top of each stem. Brace petals with pink icing, if necessary.

Hibiscus are white with pink veins, vermilion red, light, silvery pink, crimson red, and bright scarlet.

CALENDULAS (MARIGOLDS)

Fold waxed paper and cut out circles that are 2 inches in diameter. Slash circles from edge to center (Fig. 72*a*). Brush soft shortening in the hollow part of a No. 8 shallow nail; form a shallow waxed-paper cone, fasten it together with soft shortening, and press the cone firmly against the inside surface of the nail.

Make an outer circle of narrow, ridged simple back petals with a No. 103 orange cone (Figs. 72*a,b*).

Form a mound of green icing in the center with a No. 5 cone (Fig. 72*b*). Then make a smaller circle of petals so that they partially overlap the outer circle (Fig. 72*c*). Make a small inner circle of petals so that they partially overlap the second (Fig. 72*d*).

Add small orange or yellow dots to the green center (Fig. 72*d*).

Make another complete calendula. Then make a bud with a green center and the center petals only.

Freeze the flowers for ten minutes or more. (It is usually unnecessary to dry flowers of this type. They are firm because of the multiplicity of petals.)

Drop four No. 3 green stems. Then, using a ⅜-inch V-cone of green icing, make tapered, heavily ridged or zigzag leaves

(p. 44) on each long leaf stem. (Put three at the top, two in the middle, and two at the lower part of the stem.) Touch up stems and leaves with brush and light-brown vegetable color.

Remove the papers from the frozen flowers and the bud and place blossoms a little above the ends of flower stems. Add more green icing to the base of the bud and each flower so that they are joined to the stems. Bend the edges of outside petals slightly downward as soon as they thaw enough.

This type of calendula is the marigold mentioned by Shakespeare and other writers. It is orange, lemon yellow, and canary yellow. The flower is somewhat flat on top in comparison with dahlias and similar flowers (pp. 166 f.). This makes it necessary to use a shallow nail instead of a flat No. 7 nail for flowers of this type.

GLADIOLI

Using a No. 194 white cone and a No. 8 shallow nail with a 2-inch square of waxed paper cut at the corners (Fig. 73*a*) or with a shallow cone of waxed paper (Fig. 72*a*), make a spot of icing in the center and then make a short extended-back petal (Fig. 73*b* and frontispiece).

Make a second short extended-back petal a short distance to the right of the first petal (Fig. 73*c*); then a *long* extended-back petal so that it overlaps the first two petals (Fig. 73*d*). Now make two long extended-back petals so that they overlap the bottom edges of the first two (Fig. 73*e*), one long extended-back petal so that it overlaps the inside edges of the fourth and fifth petals (Fig. 73*f*). Point the petals with your fingers before or after freezing, bending the point of the top petal downward.

Make eight flowers and freeze them for ten minutes or more.

Different flowers on the same stalk will vary in construction. All will have six petals, but the proportion of long and short petals varies from flower to flower, and so does the overlapping

FIGURE 72

and underlapping of petals. The gladioli at the lower part of the stalk will be more open than the rest.

Make two large vertical leaves (pp. 45–47) with a ½-inch V-cone of green icing. Then make a long vertical stalk, starting with a No. 5 cone of light-green icing at the base and finishing with a No. 3 cone toward the top. Draw a short No. 3 stem out of the main stalk and to the left.

Make a bud at the end of the short stem with No. 104 white cone and three or four low-angled simple center petals that overlap each other. Add a light-yellow-green husk at the base of the bud and other flowers (wherever it shows) with a No. 3 cone and leaf pressure technique. Make the third bud from top right in a similar way. Make the rest of the buds with bulb technique and No. 3 yellow-green cone.

Remove the frozen gladioli from the papers and place them close together in arrangement. Overlap some flowers, and close some of them partially when they start to thaw. Put the smallest ones toward top.

In the center of each gladiolus make a white pistil with a No. 2 cone. (The pistil is divided into three parts.) Make three white stamens with the same cone; touch the top of each stamen with a brush with dark-blue or black vegetable color (Fig. 73*g*).

Gladioli are white, yellow, orange, red, lavender, purple, and intermediate shades. They are most often referred to as "glads," an affectionate nickname.

There is no need to dry these flowers or others that grow in closely clustered one-sided spikes. They look more natural if the composition of petals becomes irregular as the frozen flowers thaw.

PETUNIAS

Practice making a No. 104 white, ridged extended-back petal (pp. 115 f.) against a flat surface (Fig. 74*a* and frontispiece). Overlap the first petal with a second ridged extended-back

FIGURE 73

petal, and continue in this manner until five petals are formed (Figs. 74*b–e*).

Now make the same flower in a shallow waxed-paper cone in a No. 8 shallow nail (Fig. 74*f*). Add several fine dots of yellow-green icing to the center. Make up four more flowers in shallow waxed-paper cones and freeze them for five to ten minutes.

Drop two No. 3 green stems and draw small, short flower stems from the main ones with the same cone. Add tapered leaves with a 3/16-inch V-cone.

Make a green bud at the top of the arrangement with a No. 3 green cone. Now make the partially open bud at left center with a No. 104 white cone and several low-angled simple center petals.

Remove the frozen flowers from the papers and place them about ½ inch above the ends of the short flower stems. With a No. 4 cone of soft white icing and bulb technique, form a cone at the base of each flower (Fig. 74*g*). Smooth the surface where icing joins with water and brush, knife, or finger.

With a ⅛-inch V-cone, add sepals to the base of each flower and bud (Fig. 74*h*). Gently bend the edges of petals downward with your fingers as soon as the frozen flowers thaw sufficiently.

Petunias are white, pink, red, lavender, purple, or striped. The morning-glories that were made by the star pop-up method (pp. 13 ff.) can also be made by the shallow-nail method, which is also excellent for many other cone-shaped flowers.

FULL NASTURTIUMS

See the frontispiece for an illustration of nasturtiums in color.

Brush a thin layer of soft shortening on the inside of a No. 8 shallow nail, and place inside it a shallow cone made from a waxed-paper circle 2¾ inches in diameter (cut as illustrated in Fig. 75*a*) and press it firmly into place.

Using a No. 104 yellow cone, make five ridged extended-back

FIGURE 74

petals as shown in Figures 75*b,c.* (After the first one, begin each succeeding petal slightly under the edge of the preceding petal.)

Starting just a little below the spot where the petals separate, push the icing down toward the center of the flower with a nail or similar tool. Remove excess icing. (Fig. 75*d.* This will leave five open spaces between the petals, near the center.)

Make five nasturtiums and freeze them for ten minutes or more.

Drop No. 3 irregularly curved green stems, one for each flower and bud, so that some of the stems overlap each other. Add buds with a No. 104 yellow cone, making three or more low-angled simple center petals. Form sepals and spurs of buds with a No. 3 green cone. (Notice that the spur of a flower or a bud continues back of the stem; the stem is between the spur and the front of the flower.) Using a No. 104 green cone and the technique shown on pp. 43 f., make wavy, circular leaves on the individual stems.

Take the papers off the frozen flowers and place the flowers at the tops of flower stems. Add spurs to the base of the flowers with a No. 5 cone of soft icing (Fig. 75*e*). Now paint the inside surfaces of the flower petals delicately with fine brush and red color.

As soon as the flowers begin to thaw, bend the top edges of the petals downward slightly (Fig. 75*e*). After flowers are completed, use a nail as in Figure 75*d* to open still more the spaces between petals lying against the surface.

HALF-NASTURTIUMS

The half-nasturtium can be made directly and quickly against the surface of a cake.

Drop several irregular, wavy No. 3 green stems for flowers and leaves. Make wavy, circular leaves with a No. 125 flower tube of light green, purple-green, or variegated purple and green icing (pp. 54–59).

Add flowers by the method shown in Figures 76 *a–d.*

FIGURE 75

FIGURE 76

Pipe a mound of icing with a No. 3 yellow cone (Fig. 76*a*), and make a No. 103 yellow, ridged extended-back petal (pp. 115 f.) over the mound of yellow icing (Fig. 76*b*). Pipe four more mounds of yellow icing in a circle; cover each with a No. 103 yellow, ridged extended-back petal (Fig. 76*c*). Make No. 3

yellow lines from the base of the petals to the center of flower
(Fig. 76d).

Add spurs to the nasturtiums by inserting a No. 5 cone under
the edge of the petals one at a time, exerting pressure, and then
gradually decreasing pressure as the cone is brought out from
under the petal. (See completed flowers in the arrangement.)

Nasturtiums are yellow, orange, red, and mahogany. Brush
fine lines of red color on inside of petals if you wish.

The full nasturtium (pp. 192–94) is more realistic, but there
is also a time and a place for flowers like the half-nasturtium.
If you have only a few minutes in which to work, or if you
are making a low-priced item on a production basis, direct
flowers are often the answer. Furthermore, most of the flowers
that will stay on the side of a cake without propping are those
that are made directly against the cake.

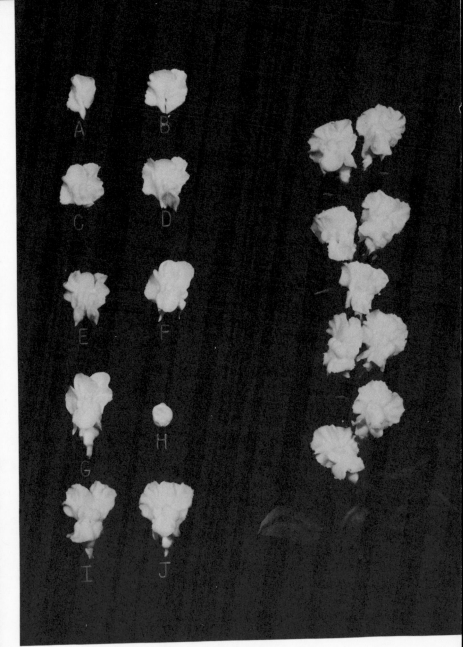

FIGURE 77

CHAPTER XIV

Flowers Made by Metal-Surface Technique

YOU HAVE already used the metal-surface technique for many flowers in preceding chapters; it was often an alternate method that you chose because of its convenience. In this chapter you will find that metal-surface technique is used in a very special way for full tulips and iris. Indeed, we are not aware of any other method that could be used for buttercream-flower construction of this type. The snapdragons, however, can be made directly against a cake.

SNAPDRAGONS

Make the arrangement of main stem and leaves (Fig. 77), and place a small mound of white icing one inch from the main stem wherever you wish to make a flower. Make the No. 103 white extended-back petals shown in Figures 77a,b, so that they go up and over the mound of icing, as for half-nasturtiums (pp. 194–97).

Using No. 103 and No. 3 white cones, make the rest of the petals shown in Figures 77c–g. Draw short stem from the base of the flower to the main stem; add small green sepals shown in Figure 77j.

The direct method just described is not much faster than the metal-surface technique, but the latter makes it possible for us to tilt the snapdragons at more graceful and natural angles. (The frontispiece includes a color arrangement of snapdragons.)

Using a No. 103 white cone against a metal surface, make *two-thirds* of a long, wavy extended-back petal (Fig. 77a), using a low angle and an extreme right tilt.

Make a dozen or more at a time. Achieve the first step for all of them, allowing space enough between petals for the complete flowers. Then do the second step for all of them, then the third, and so on. Turn the metal surface around before working on Figure 77*f*; complete the same petal on all flowers; then turn the metal surface back to its original position for the final petal in Figure 77*g*.

Placing the tube under the right edge of the first petal and, at the top of the flower, make the last *one-half* of a long, wavy extended back petal (Fig. 77*b*). Then, using a No. 3 cone of soft white icing and bulb technique, make two or three forward-and-back movements on the lower part of the first two petals (Fig. 77*c*).

Placing the base of a No. 103 white cone ¼-inch below the flower and to the right of center, pointing the tube to the left and using a high angle with a little right tilt, make a short extended-center petal. (Fig. 77*d*. Cover the lower half of the bulb work [Fig. 77*c*] with this and the next two petals.)

Placing the base of a No. 103 white cone ¼ inch below the flower and to the left of center, pointing the tube to the right and using a high angle with a little left tilt, make a short extended-center petal. (Fig. 77*e*. The last two petals form an upside-down V, but they do *not* come together.)

Turn the metal surface around. Placing the base of a No. 103 white cone at the center of the bulb work (Fig. 77*c*), make a narrow simple back petal so that it meets or covers the top edges of the two extended-center petals (Fig. 77*f*). Turn the metal surface back to its original position.

Using a No. 3 cone of soft white icing and bulb technique, placing the tube against the metal surface under the last petal and, moving the tube from left to right and back again, make a thin formation between the two extended-center petals.

Then make a narrow, high, shell-like formation that partially covers the bottom part of the thin formation previously made and finishes in a short, narrow line against the surface and considerably below the rest of the flower (Fig. 77g).

Make and freeze several flowers for four or five minutes or more.

Use latticing technique (DC 56)* to form a long, straight No. 3 green stem. Draw short stems for large leaves at the base of the main stem with a No. 2 green cone. Add green buds at the top of the main stem with a No. 3 green cone and bulb technique.

Form small, narrow leaves with No. 3 green cone and leaf pressure technique (pp. 41 ff.). Then make two short, small leaves with the same cone and technique at the base of each leaf stem. Using a ⅜-inch V-cone, form large tapered leaves at ends of small stems. Make the center leaf on a metal surface, freeze it, and then form it over a ball of green icing as it thaws (p. 53).

Make mounds of icing with a No. 3 white cone wherever the centers of the flowers are to be placed (Fig. 77h), allowing space enough for the small stem between the flower and the main stem.

Remove the frozen flowers from the metal surface with a thin, sharp knife and place the centers of the flowers against the mounds of white icing (Fig. 77i), tilting the flowers at various angles.

Draw a short, small stem from the bottom of each flower to the main stem with a No. 2 green cone. Using the same No. 2 green cone and leaf pressure technique, make one sepal just below white base of each flower (Fig. 77j). Then make two sepals (one below the other) against the left side of the white base, and make two more sepals (one below the other) against the right side of the white base. (The sixth sepal, in back of the flower, is not shown.)

Sepals are made in a similar manner against the green buds at the top of the main stem.

---

* "DC" indicates pages in *Decorating Cakes for Fun and Profit;* "27C," pages in *27 Special Creations for Cake Decorators.*

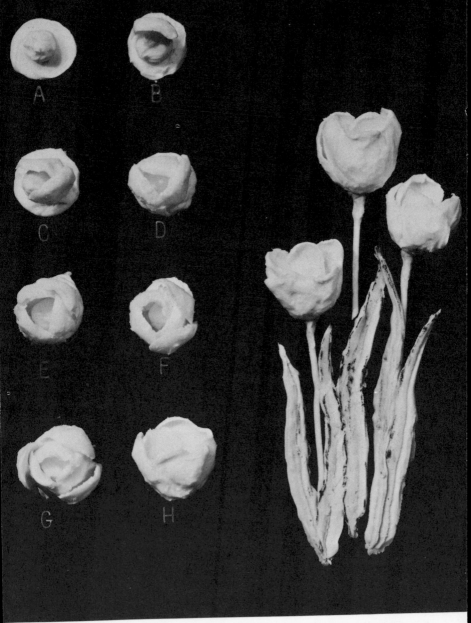

FIGURE 78

As soon as the flowers begin to thaw, gently bend the top petals downward toward the cake surface to hide the mounds of icing and to give a "popcorn" look to the snapdragons (Fig. 77*j*).

Snapdragons are white, pink, red, yellow, and intermediate shades. The snapdragon is a complex flower, but well worth learning. It adds vitality and zest to a decoration.

FULL TULIPS

See the red tulips in the frontispiece.

Using a dry metal surface (preferably a flat can of liquid ice or similar product, (see pp. 203 ff.) and a No. 125 white cone, make several rows of medium-angled extended-back petals (pp. 115 f.). If you do not have a flat can of liquid ice or a similar product, use two metal surfaces alternately, keeping one in the freezing compartment while the other is being used in the room.) Place the metal surface and petals in a freezing compartment for five minutes or more.

On an unglazed cardboard, make several round wafers of icing about ¼-inch thick and one inch in diameter. (Fig. 78*a*. That is, using a No. 5 cone of white icing, make a circle and then fill in the center.) Using a No. 5 white cone and bulb technique, make a mound of icing that is about ½-inch in height and ½-inch in diameter on the center of each wafer (Fig. 78*a*).

Loosen a few frozen petals from the metal surface with a thin, sharp knife but leave them on the metal surface so that they will stay cold until you are ready to use them. Put the pointed base of one of the petals into a wafer ¼-inch inside its circumference, and the cupped side of the petal facing the center mound of icing (Fig. 78*b*).

Place a second petal in a similar way, but overlap the right edge of the first petal (Fig. 78*c*). Then add a third petal in the same way, but overlap the edges of the first and second petals.

(Fig. 78*d*. If your fingers become sticky, rub them with a dry towel now and then.)

Add three outside petals so that they overlap the spots where the first three inner petals overlap each other (Figs. 78*e–g*).

Make up the rest of the tulips.

Let some outside petals overlap each other slightly, others not at all. If outside petals will not stay up against inside petals, add an additional and higher No. 5 ring of white icing around the top edge of the wafer.

If petals are obviously cupped too deeply or not deeply enough, so that they will not fit together well, then make a new batch of petals at a different angle that will correct the problem. Petals made at a lower angle are more shallow and work better when they are used as outside petals; those made at a medium angle are less shallow and work better when used as inside petals.

If the petals become too soft to handle, freeze them again before continuing.

Make three straight stems with a No. 5 green cone. Using a ⅜-inch V-cone and vertical leaf technique (pp. 45–47), form several leaves that start from the base of the stem.

After the flowers have dried on unglazed cardboard for a few minutes until they are no longer sticky (or for a few hours or overnight, if you prefer), cut away the excess icing at the base of each tulip with a knife (Fig. 78*h*), tilt the flower on its side, and press and shape its base with your fingers until it is round and smooth. (Smooth the rounded surface with a moist brush, if necessary.)

Shape the rest of the tulips and set them upright on unglazed cardboard. Point the tips of the petals slightly between thumb and finger for some varieties of tulips, and move petals to desired angles before they become completely dry.

Using a No. 2 white cone and cone star technique, place the

opening of the tube below the surface of the mound in the bottom of the tulip and bring a stamen upward. Make six stamens and brush the tops with dark-blue or black vegetable color. (Stamens are shown in frontispiece, but not in Fig. 78.)

Place tulips on their sides at the tops of three stems.

Tulips are white, yellow, pink, red, purple, intermediate shades, and various combinations of colors. A fast method for making half-tulips on the top or side of a cake is given on pp. 131–34.

A good way to show off full tulips is to make the tulip leaves and stems on the side of a cake. Then place full tulips at the top edge of the cake, and at the top of the stems.

Miniature tulips are easier to make than the large ones. They are appropriate for small cakes and for garden scenes on large cakes.

IRIS

See the iris in the frontispiece and also Figure 79.

Using a dry metal surface (preferably a flat can of liquid ice or similar product, see pp. 203 ff.) and a No. 104 white cone, make up several rows of wavy-back petals (pp. 115 f.) with ½-inch extensions. (If you do not have a flat can of liquid ice or a similar product, use two metal surfaces alternately, keeping one in the freezing compartment while the other is being used in the room.) Place the metal surface in freezing compartment for five minutes or more.

Drop two long No. 3 green stems (Fig. 79); then draw two very short No. 3 stems for buds.

Make the buds with a No. 5 green cone and bulb technique, and add a small bit of white to each green bud with a No. 104 cone. Then make tan husks on the buds and stems with No. 3 cone and leaf-pressure technique (DC 29, 39 ff.).

Using a ⅜-inch V-cone and vertical leaf technique (pp. 45–47), make long green leaves from the base of the stems. Touch up the leaves with a brush and light-brown vegetable color.

Make a mound of soft white icing ½-inch above the top of the stem with a No. 5 cone. (Fig. 79*a*. The mound should be about ⅜-inch in depth and diameter.)

Loosen a few frozen petals from the metal surface with a thin, sharp knife, but leave them on the metal so that they will stay cold until you are ready to use them. Place the base of one petal in the mound of soft white icing, on the side opposite you, with the petal wavy side up and flat against the surface (Fig. 79*b*).

Place the base of a No. 104 white cone into the center of the mound and form a simple center petal (medium angle and no tilt) to indicate small petals at the center of the flower (Fig. 79*b*.)

Place a second large frozen petal on edge, with the wavy surface on the outside and the base in the mound of soft icing; point the petal to the left edge of the first petal (Fig. 79*c*).

Place a third large frozen petal on edge, with its wavy surface to the outside and its base in the mound of soft icing and point it to the right edge of the first petal (Fig. 79*d*).

Place a fourth petal on edge, with its wavy surface up and the base in the mound of soft icing; point it to the right and slightly downward from the center mound of icing (Fig. 79*e*.)

Place a fifth petal on edge, with the wavy surface up and its base in the mound of soft icing, pointing the petal to the left and slightly downward from the center mound (Fig. 79*f*).

Now add another ball of white icing on top of the first mound, between the fourth and fifth petals (Fig. 79*f*). Place a horizontal sixth petal pointing toward you in a position that is vertical to the surface, with the wavy surface up and the base in the *first* mound of soft icing (Fig. 79*g*).

Make a tan husk at the base of the flower and against the stem with a No. 3 cone and leaf pressure technique.

As soon as the sixth petal begins to thaw, bend it downward slightly so that it rests on top of the second ball of icing (Fig.

FIGURE 79

79*g*). And as soon as they thaw sufficiently, bend the first, second, and third petals so that the tops touch, overlap slightly, or almost touch each other (Fig. 79*h*).

Form stamens on the upper surfaces of the three lower petals so that they taper as they come out from the center. Use a No. 13 star tube of yellow or orange icing and back-away bead technique, which is similar to back-away leaf technique (Fig. 79*h*; see p. 52).

Make another iris at the top of the second stem.

Irises are white, blue, purple, pink, yellow, red, and various combinations. Irises can be used effectively against the side of a cake as well as on top. They can also be used on the top edge of a cake, as suggested for full tulips (pp. 203 ff).

If your fingers become sticky while you are making iris or full tulips, rub them with a dry towel now and then. The metal surfaces and the knife blade used for loosening the petals must also be kept as dry as possible.

If petals become too soft to handle, freeze them again before continuing.

This method of making flowers will seem very time-consuming when you try it for the first time, but practice will soon give you the knack of it. Some graduate students are able to make the iris arrangement in ten or fifteen minutes from the time they start making petals against a metal surface.

Chapter XV

Flowers Made by Cut-out Method

THE CUT-OUT METHOD of making buttercream flowers as taught in this chapter will be easy for those who have had experience with gum paste. The soft texture of buttercream icing gives the flowers a very natural appearance.

Large calla lilies and large orchids are not used very often, but it is good to be able to produce them when they are appropriate. Until now, they have been made with gum paste, marzipan, royal icing, and pulled sugar.

Making large buttercream flowers by the cut-out method demonstrates the practicality of the technique. Any flower smaller than those in Figures 80, 81, and 83 is quite naturally easier to make; half-sized and smaller flowers, for instance, require neither a waxed-paper cone nor air-drying; they can be used on a cake as soon as they are formed.

Small calla lilies and orchids (in color on frontispiece) can be made not only by the cut-out method but also by the basic-petal technique, using direct method, metal-surface technique, or a combination of the two. The basic petals can also be combined with petals made by the cut-out method.

LARGE CALLA LILIES

Work enough sifted powdered sugar (confectioner's or icing sugar) into some buttercream icing to make it handle like putty or modeling clay. It must not be sticky when you start to roll it out. Work each portion smooth again before you start to form it on the board. It is possible to add too much powdered sugar; then it will crack before you can shape it properly.

Color a very small portion yellow for the centers of calla lilies. Color a small amount green for calla leaves, and leave the rest white. Cover each portion of icing so that it will not dry before you are ready to use it.

Cut in half several waxed-paper circles 7 inches in diameter. Make each half-circle into a narrow cone with the point at the center of the diameter (Fig. 80*a*) and the top of the cone about 1¼ inches in diameter. Seal cone with a piece of Scotch tape or paper clip, and stuff pieces of paper towel into cone to keep it from collapsing when it is in use. (These cones can be kept and reused many times for large calla lilies and orchids.)

Make a waxed-paper or parchment-paper pattern shaped like the icing in Figure 80*b*. (The original measurements were 5 by 2¾ inches.) Dust the bench or board with corn starch.

Open the tightly closed container, take out a piece of stiff white buttercream icing about the size of an egg, and work it smooth. (Add more sifted powdered sugar if the icing is sticky.) Flatten the icing against the dusted board; roll it out evenly with a small rolling pin as though it were pie crust until it is ⅛ inch thick.

Place the pattern on top of the rolled-out icing and cut around the pattern with a sharp paring knife. Remove paper and excess icing (Fig. 80*b*). Put excess icing back in the tightly covered container; it can be worked into the fresh icing and reused.

Pinch the edges of the lower two-thirds of the flower to give illusion of thinness; dust lower half of flower with corn starch (Fig. 80*c*).

Place the point of the waxed-paper cone at the base of the lily. Bring the right edge of the petal up and part way over the cone (Fig. 80*d*). Bring the left edge of petal up to overlap the right edge; press lightly, but do not seal the edges together (Fig. 80*e*). Turn the lily upside down on unglazed cardboard. Pinch the

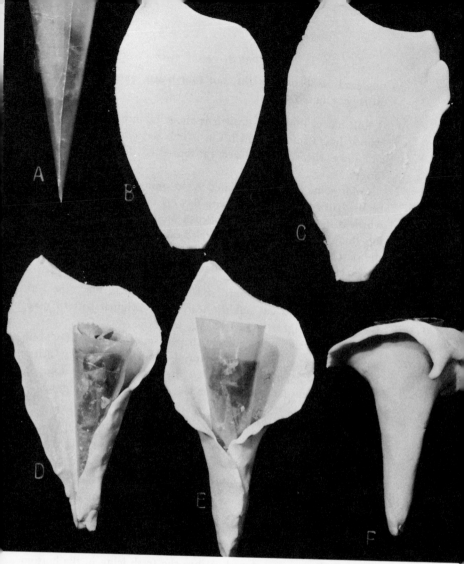

FIGURE 80

top edges so that they are thin. Then curl the thin edges back
and downward slightly (Fig. 80f). Loosen the waxed-paper cone
gently; then replace it lightly.

Make three or more calla lilies and allow them to air-dry on unglazed cardboard for three or four hours, or overnight, if the air is very humid.

Roll out yellow icing until it is about ¼ inch in diameter and shaped like a smooth pencil. Cut it into sections 2¼ inches long and place them on unglazed cardboard to dry three hours or longer.

Color some coarse granulated sugar orange-yellow. (This will be used to represent the minute flowers that cover the spadix—which is the calla-lily center.) Brush some thin orange-yellow icing along the sides and tops of *dried* calla-lily centers. Then cover the centers with coarse orange-yellow granulated sugar. (Fig. 81. Excess colored sugar can be reused.)

Roll out green icing until it is ⅛ inch thick. Place the leaf pattern on it and cut out the leaf. (The original pattern used for leaves in Fig. 81 was 4 by 3¼ inches.)

Place the leaf on irregularly shaped small mounds of waxed paper so that it will have a natural appearance when it dries. Pinch the edges of leaves so that they are thin. Make four or more leaves and let them dry for several hours or overnight.

Drop separate stems for leaves and lilies with a No. 5 cone of green icing. (Fig. 81. Stems can also be made by rolling out thin strips of the same green icing that is used for leaves.) Place a leaf at the right.

Remove the waxed-paper cones from the lilies and place the lilies at the tops of the stems. Brush some thin, light green icing on the base of the flowers and into the top part of the stems.

Place the rest of leaves at the ends of leaf stems.

Put some fresh white icing in the bottom of each lily. Insert the orange-yellow center (spadix) into the fresh icing in the bottom of each calla lily (Fig. 81).

Calla lilies are white, yellow, and pink. The large calla-lily arrangement could be used only on the top of a very large cake, or it could be used without stems at the base of a very large

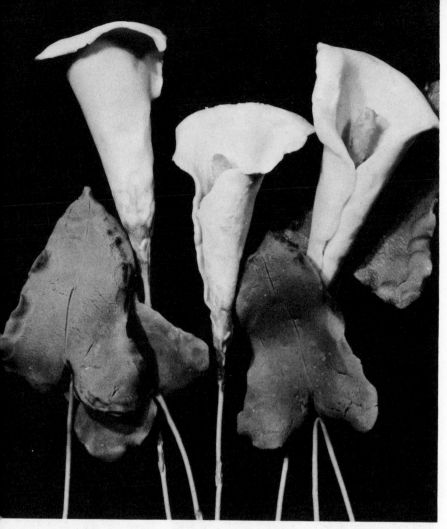

FIGURE 81

cake. You will make smaller lilies most of the time. Remember to reduce all measurements in the same proportion—leaves, stems, and centers as well as the flowers themselves. Roll the icing two-thirds as thick.

Small calla lilies (half-size or smaller) can be made very rapidly with the cut-out method. Several can be cut out at one

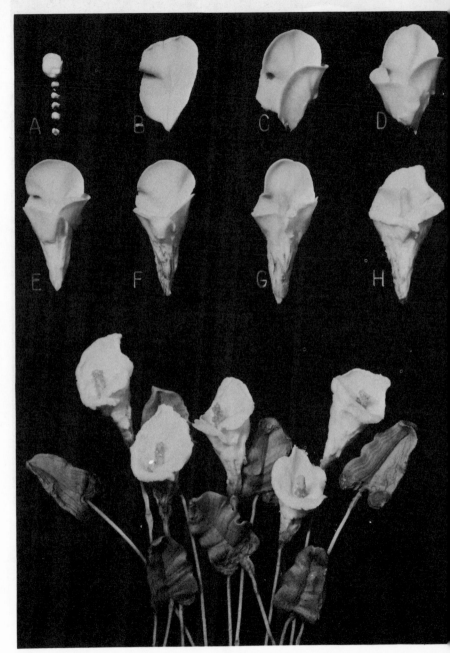

FIGURE 82

time with a homemade cookie cutter made from a tin can and soldered. Form them around a No. 3 metal tube and remove the tube as soon as they are formed. No paper cones or drying time is required. Just put the lilies on the cake as you form them, or make them all up and use them later.

Make the leaves of small calla lilies by the cut-out method or with a V-cone and a No. 3 cone, as in Figure 82. Make the centers by the cut-out method or with a tube and metal-surface technique, as in Figure 82. Drop stems with a No. 3 green cone.

Calla lilies are used frequently on wedding cakes, confirmation cakes, and Easter cakes. They are very effective in corsage and basket arrangements.

SMALL CALLA LILIES

Using a No. 5 white cone, form a ball of icing at the top of an imagined one-inch vertical line (Fig. 82*a*). Then with a No. 125 white cone, make a high-angled back petal with a one-inch extension (pp. 115 f.). Make the top of the petal go up and over the ball of icing and keep the edges of the petal off the surface (Fig. 82*b*).

Placing the tube at a low angle under the right edge of the back petal and tilting the tube to the extreme right, make an overlapping center petal (p. 103), tilting the tube to the extreme left just before finishing the petal (Fig. 82*c*). In a similar way, make an overlapping center petal at the left of the back petal, overlapping to the right of the first center petal and tilting the tube to the extreme right just before finishing (Fig. 82*d*).

Using bulb technique and a No. 5 white cone, lengthen the base of the lily (Fig. 82*e*) and smooth the base with a moist brush. Brush very thin light-green icing or light-green vegetable color on the base (Fig. 82*f*).

Make the center with a No. 5 orange-yellow cone. (Fig. 82*g*. An alternate and more realistic method is given later in the description of the small-calla-lily arrangement.)

After the flower has air-dried for ten minutes or more and is no longer sticky, shape the top of lily with your fingers into a characteristic curved point. Then roll the top edges outward and downward. (Use starch or water on your fingers if the icing is too sticky.)

Drop green stems with a No. 3 cone, having some stems cross others. Then add green leaves with a ½-inch V-cone and a No. 3 cone using special technique on p. 60.

Flowers can be made by the direct method described above and illustrated in Figures 82*a–h*. The flowers in the illustrated arrangement were made with metal-surface technique so that they can be tilted at different angles.

If you wish to use metal-surface technique for flowers, omit step in Figure 82*a*.

Complete the steps in Figures 82*b–e*; freeze the flowers for five minutes or longer; then remove frozen flowers from the metal surface with a sharp paring knife and place them at various angles on small white mounds of icing.

Brush very light green coloring on base of each flower (Fig. 82*f*). When the flowers start to thaw, shape them as in Figure 82*h*.

Make ½-inch long cylindrical centers on a dry metal surface with a No. 5 orange-yellow cone. Cover them with orange-yellow coarse granulated sugar; remove excess sugar by tilting the metal surface and hitting the edge of it with a knife handle; and freeze the centers for three minutes or more. Remove the frozen centers with a sharp knife. Place some of them in the bottom of the lilies so that they do not touch the sides of the lilies, and put the rest of them on unglazed cardboard, dry them, and then store them for future use.

Calla lilies are white, yellow, and pink. Small calla lilies can be made quickly with either the direct or the metal-surface

technique. You will find many uses for these and the small calla
lilies made with the cut-out method.

LARGE ORCHIDS

Study the method for the large calla lily, pp. 209–15.

Knead sifted powdered sugar into some white buttercream icing,
or add it to some icing in a mixing machine, until the icing is
the consistency of putty and no longer sticky. Dust a board with
corn starch. Then take a small amount of thickened icing, place
it on the board, dust it with corn starch, and roll it out with a
small rolling pin as though you were rolling out pie crust, until
it is ⅛ inch thick or less.

Place a paper pattern shaped like the icing illustrated in Figure
83a on top of the icing you have just rolled out. (The original
pattern was 3¼ inches long and 2¾ inches wide.) Cut around
the pattern and remove the scraps of icing. (Fig. 83a. See the
method for the large calla lily, pp. 209–15.)

Pinch the edges of the icing; place the waxed cone on top of
icing; press the edges together after they are brought to the top
of the cone; turn the flower upside down; then pinch and flute
the top edges of the slipper (center cone of orchid) as shown in
Figure 83b.

Let the slipper dry on unglazed cardboard for several hours
or overnight.

This is an alternate method that can be used instead of the
one that was used in Figure 83. Cut out two large petals like
the one in Figure 83c and three narrow petals like the one in
Figure 83d. Pinch the edges of the petals to make them thin.
Let them dry on mounds of waxed paper for several hours or
overnight.

Using a No. 125 white cone of regular buttercream decorating
icing and the metal-surface technique, make two ridged back
petals with 2-inch extensions. (Fig. 83c; see also pp. 115 f. The

original petals were 2¾ inches long and 1¾ inches wide.) Then, using a No. 70 white cone and leaf technique, make three long tapered leaflike petals against the same metal surface. (Fig. 83*d*. The original petals were 2½ inches long and ½ inch wide.) Freeze the two large and three narrow petals for ten minutes or more.

With a No. 5 cone, form a mound of white icing the size of a quarter on the top center of a cake. Put another mound of icing the size of a quarter but twice as thick as the first one to the left of center, and a similar mound to the right of center.

Remove the frozen petals from the metal surface with a sharp knife. Place the base of each narrow petal into the center mound of icing, and arrange narrow petals in an irregular pattern.

Using a No. 5 white cone, insert small amounts of icing under the narrow petals to keep them from lying flat. (When petals thaw, they will settle over these small amounts of icing in graceful folds.)

Place the two large petals so that the base of each petal is on top of the center mound of icing and the part of each petal that is nearest the center is over a high mound of icing. Bring the edges of these large petals down over the high mounds of icing as soon as they thaw so that the mounds of icing are concealed. Using a No. 5 white cone, insert small amounts of icing at various places under edges of both large petals. (When these petals thaw, they will also settle over these small amounts of icing in graceful folds.)

Remove the waxed-paper cone from the slipper and place the base of the slipper into the center mound of icing. Smooth the center of the orchid with a moist brush.

Make a very short yellow center in the bottom of the slipper with a No. 5 cone. Then paint the orchid with a fine brush and pink or orchid vegetable color. Paint the middle part of the slipper (sometimes called the throat) canary yellow.

Orchids are white, pale pink, orchid, or pale green. Try

FIGURE 83

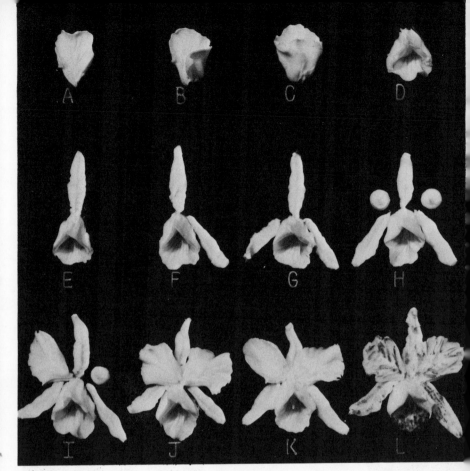

FIGURE 84

making a large bow of light-green ribbon with a No. 125 cone on the top center of cake, and add an orchid on top of the ribbon.

We have previously called attention to the fact that every part of the large orchid can be made by the cut-out method. Parts of small orchids or complete orchids can also be made by the cut-out method.

The following method of making small orchids depends entirely upon basic petal and leaf techniques. Small orchids can be made directly on the cake (top or side); the slippers and large petals can be made on a metal surface, frozen, and then formed into small orchids on top of a cake.

SMALL ORCHIDS

Using a No. 104 white cone, make a high-angled, ridged back petal that is extended forward ½ inch (Fig. 84*a*; see pp. 115 f.).

Holding a No. 125 white cone at a very low angle and at an extreme right tilt, place the edge of the tube under the right edge of first petal. Bring the tube to a high angle and straight above the center of the first petal (Fig. 84*b*). Holding the same cone at a very low angle and at an extreme left tilt, place the edge of the tube under the left edge of first petal and bring the tube to a high angle and straight above the center of the first petal, so that left edge of second petal and right edge of third petal touch each other (Fig. 84*c*).

After making the first three petals, turn the surface halfway around (Fig. 84*d*). Using a ⅛-inch V-cone of white icing, make three narrow, tapered leaflike petals that start at the base of the slipper and are approximately 1¼ inches long (Figs. 84*e-g*).

Using a No. 3 white cone, put a ball of icing to the left of the top narrow petal and another to the right of it (Fig. 84*h*) to keep the next two petals from being too flat. Then make a *No. 104* white ridged back petal extending from the base of the slipper ½ inch forward and over the ball of icing at left (Fig. 84*i*), followed by a No. 104 ridged back petal to the right in a similar way (Fig. 84*j*).

Make a short light-yellow center in the bottom of the slipper with a No. 3 cone (Fig. 84*k*). Paint the orchid with a fine brush and pink or orchid vegetable color, and paint the middle part of the slipper (or throat) canary yellow (Fig. 84*l*).

Drop a long, irregularly curved diagonal No. 3 green stem (Fig. 85). Make short, small stems at intervals on either side of the long stem and add orchids as described on this page and illustrated in Figure 84.

Leave some orchids white, except for the canary yellow in the middle of the throat; color others more or less with pink or orchid. Orchids can also be made with delicate pink or orchid icing in the beginning and then brushed with a darker shade of the same color.

Make some large petals and slippers on a metal surface and freeze them. Remove the frozen petals and dry them on unglazed cardboard overnight. Then place dried slippers and large petals upright in a center ball of icing. (Notice the two flowers in foreground. Little or no support is needed.)

Orchids are white, pale pink, orchid, or light green.

Ice the top of a cake with very pale-green icing and make the arrangement in Figure 85 against this pale-green background. Make small slippers and large petals by the cut-out method and let them dry until they are firm. Then put slipper, or slipper and large petals, upright in centers of small orchids.

Let us remind you of the Color Index of Flowers on pp. 225 ff., which will help you to find the right flowers to fit your color scheme. Now and then the Flowers of the Months (pp. 228 f.) and the State Flowers (pp. 230 f.) will help you to decide what flowers to put on a particular cake. The Index (pp. 237 ff.) is very detailed and includes many references to *Decorating Cakes for Fun and Profit* and to *27 Special Creations for Cake Decorators.* When you do not understand a technical term in the text, or when you wish to look up a particular topic or name, turn to the index for help in finding what you need when you need it.

FIGURE 85

Color Index of Flowers

BLUE

Ageratum, 40
Bluebell, 29
Crocus, 75 f.
Forget-me-not, 145–48
Gentian, 77 f.
Hyacinth, 15
Iris, 205–208
Lilac, 14 f.

Monkshood, 134 f.
Morning-glory, 22 f.
Pansy, 156 f.
Sweet Pea, 120–25
Veronica, 15
Vetch, 117 f.
Violet, 150 ff.

BRONZE

Blanketflower (Gaillardia), 54–56
Cat-Tail, 63 f.

Chrysanthemum, 82–86
Nasturtium, 49

CREAM

Chrysanthemum, 82–86
Daylily, 91 f.
Hollyhock, 27 f.

WHITE

Mistletoe, 64 f.
Pussy-Willow, 63
Sweet Pea, 120–25

GREEN

Orchid, 217 ff.

Shamrock, DC 83

LAVENDER

Bluebell, 29
Butterfly Bush, 13

Canterbury Bell, 23
Cottage Pink, 153 f.

LAVENDER (CONT.)

Crocus, 75 f.
Field Daisy, 80 f.
Gladiolus, 188–90
Hyacinth, 15
Lilac, 14 f.
Orchid, 217 ff.

Pansy, 156 f.
Petunia, 190–92
Sweet Pea, 120–25
Vetch, 117 f.
Wisteria, 118–20

MAROON

Blanketflower (Gaillardia),
    154–56
Dahlia, 166–68
Daylily, 91 f.

Hollyhock, 27 f.
Peony, 173 ff.
Tulip, 203 ff.

ORANGE

Calendula (Marigold), 187 f.
Gladiolus, 188–90

Nasturtium, 192 ff.
Pumpkin, DC 86

PINK

Apple Blossom, 136 ff.
Bleeding Heart, 34–36
Bluebell, 29
Calla Lily, 209 ff.
Canterbury Bell, 18 ff.
Carnation, 175 ff.
Chrysanthemum, 82 ff.
Cottage Pink, 153 f.
Daffodil, 165 f.
Dahlia, 166–68
Daylily, 91 f.
Field Daisy, 80 f.
Hibiscus, 184 ff.
Hollyhock, 27 f.

Hyacinth, 15
Iris, 205–208
Lilac, 14 f.
Monkshood, 134 f.
Orchid, 217 ff.
Peony, 173 ff.
Petunia, 190–92
Rose, 126 ff.
Snapdragon, 199 ff.
Sweet Pea, 120–25
Trailing Arbutus, 149
Tulip, 203 ff.
Wild Rose, 180 ff.
Wisteria, 118–20

PURPLE

Butterfly Bush, 13
Canterbury Bell, 18 ff.
Crocus, 75 f.
Dahlia, 166–68
Daylily, 91 f.
Gladiolus, 188–90
Hyacinth, 15

Iris, 205–208
Morning-glory, 22 f.
Pansy, 156 f.
Petunia, 190–92
Tulip, 203 ff.
Vetch, 117 f.
Violet, 150 ff.

RED

Carnation, 175 ff.
Chrysanthemum, 82 ff.
Cottage Pink, 153 f.
Dahlia, 166–68
Gladiolus, 188–90
Hibiscus, 184 ff.
Holly, 52
Hollyhock, 27 f.
Hyacinth, 15
Iris, 205–208

Morning-glory, 22 f.
Nasturtium, 192 ff.
Oriental Poppy, 32
Pansy, 156 f.
Petunia, 190–92
Rose, 126 ff.
Snapdragon, 199 ff.
Sweet Pea, 120–25
Tulip, 203 ff.

SCARLET

Bittersweet, 64
Hibiscus, 184 ff.
Honeysuckle, 39 f.

Oriental Poppy, 32
Poinsettia, DC 43

WHITE

Apple Blossom, 136 ff.
Bleeding Heart, 34–36
Calla Lily, 209 ff.
Canterbury Bell, 18 ff.
Carnation, 175 ff.
Christmas Rose, 182 ff.

Chrysanthemum, 82 ff.
Cottage Pink, 153 f.
Crocus, 75 f.
Daffodil, 165 f.
Dahlia, 166–68
Dogwood, 158–61

WHITE (CONT.)

Easter Lily, 88 ff.
Forget-Me-Not, 145–48
Gardenia, 25–27
Gladiolus, 188–90
Hibiscus, 184 ff.
Hollyhock, 27 f.
Hyacinth, 15
Iris, 205–208
Lily-of-the-Valley, DC 43
Monkshood, 134 f.
Morning-glory, 22 f.
Narcissus, 163 ff.
Orchid, 217 ff.
Pansy, 156 f.
Peony, 173 ff.

Petunia, 190–92
Poinsettia, DC 43
Pussy-Willow, 63
Rose, 126 ff.
Snapdragon, 199 ff.
Snowball, 16
Snowberry, 34
Snowdrop, 76 f.
Sweet Pea, 120–25
Trailing Arbutus, 149
Tulip, 203 ff.
Vetch, 117 f.
Violet, 150 ff.
Water Lily, 168–73
Wild Rose, 180 ff.

YELLOW

Blanketflower (Gaillardia),
    154–56
Calendula (Marigold), 187 f.
Calla Lily, 209 ff.
Chrysanthemum, 82 ff.
Crocus, 75 f.
Dahlia, 166–68
Daylily, 91 f.
Field Daisy, 80 f.
Forsythia, 73 f.
Gladiolus, 188–90
Goldenrod, 16 f.

Hollyhock, 27 f.
Hyacinth, 15
Iris, 205–208
Lilac, 14 f.
Nasturtium, 192 ff.
Pansy, 156 f.
Rose, 126 ff.
Snapdragon, 199 ff.
Sunflower, 78 f.
Tulip, 203 ff.
Violet, 150 ff.
Wild Rose, 180 ff.

Flowers of the Months

JANUARY

Carnation, pp. 175 ff.   Snowdrop, pp. 76 f.

FEBRUARY

Violet, pp. 150 ff.   Primrose

MARCH

Jonquil   Daffodil, pp. 165 f.

APRIL

Sweet Pea, pp. 120–25   Daisy, pp. 80 f.

MAY

Lily of the Valley, DC 43   Hawthorne

JUNE

Rose, 126 ff.; DC 49   Honeysuckle, pp. 39 f.

JULY

Larkspur   Water Lily, pp. 168–73

AUGUST

Poppy, pp. 34–36   Gladiolus, pp. 188–90

Appendix C

State Flowers

ALABAMA	Goldenrod	pp. 16 f.
ARIZONA	Saguaro Cactus	p. 66
ARKANSAS	Apple Blossom	pp. 136 ff.
CALIFORNIA	Golden Poppy	
COLORADO	Columbine	27C 9
CONNECTICUT	Mountain Laurel	
DELAWARE	Peach Blossom	
FLORIDA	Orange Blossom	
GEORGIA	Cherokee Rose	
IDAHO	Syringa	
ILLINOIS	Violet	pp. 150 ff.
INDIANA	Zinnia	pp. 80 f.
IOWA	Wild Rose	pp. 180 ff.
KANSAS	Sunflower	pp. 78 f.
KENTUCKY	Goldenrod	pp. 16 f.
LOUISIANA	Magnolia	
MAINE	Pine Cone	
MARYLAND	Black-eyed Susan	
MASSACHUSETTS	Mayflower	
MICHIGAN	Apple Blossom	pp. 136 ff.
MINNESOTA	Moccasin Flower	
MISSISSIPPI	Magnolia Grandiflora	
MISSOURI	Hawthorn	
MONTANA	Bitterroot	
NEBRASKA	Goldenrod	pp. 16 f.

231

NEVADA	Sagebrush	
NEW HAMPSHIRE	Purple Lilac	pp. 14 f.
NEW JERSEY	Violet	pp. 150 ff.
NEW MEXICO	Yucca	
NEW YORK	Rose	pp. 180 ff.; DC 49
NORTH CAROLINA	Dogwood	pp. 158–61
NORTH DAKOTA	Wild Prairie Rose	
OHIO	Scarlet Carnation	pp. 175 ff.
OKLAHOMA	Mistletoe	pp. 64 f.
OREGON	Oregon Grape	
PENNSYLVANIA	Mountain Laurel	
RHODE ISLAND	Violet	pp. 150 ff.
SOUTH CAROLINA	Yellow Jessamine	
SOUTH DAKOTA	Anemone	
TENNESSEE	Iris	pp. 205–208
TEXAS	Bluebonnet	
UTAH	Sego Lily	
VERMONT	Red Clover	
VIRGINIA	American Dogwood	pp. 158–61
WASHINGTON	Rhododendron	
WEST VIRGINIA	Rhododendron	
WISCONSIN	Violet	pp. 150 ff.
WYOMING	Indian Paintbrush	

Equipment and Materials
Needed for Flowers*

Metal Tubes: Nos. 1, 2, 3, 4, 5, 13, 27, 30, 101s, 101, 102, 103,
    104, 125, 70, 79, 81, 93
Flower Nails: Nos. 7, 8, 12
Refrigerator or Deep-Freeze
Liquid Ice (flat cans)

Metal Surface	Towels
Scissors	Corn Starch
Spatula	Shortening
Table Knife	Egg Whites
Paring Knife	Simple Syrup
Small Brushes	Piping Jelly
Icing Containers (air-tight)	Glamor-Glitter
Icing Pans	Water
Ruler	Unglazed Cardboard
Turntable or Lazy Susan	Parchment Paper
Small Rolling Pin	Waxed Paper
Pins	Scotch Tape
Cardboard Box	Artificial Yellow Stamens

Buttercream Decorating Icing (recipes on pp. 235–38)
Paste or Liquid Vegetable Coloring: Black, Blue, Brown,
    Green, Orange, Pink, Purple, Red, Yellow
Powdered (Confectioner's) Sugar
Granulated Sugar (coarse)

* The reader may obtain further information by addressing the
Snyder School of Cake Decoration, 16841 Grand River Avenue, Detroit
27, Michigan.

APPENDIX E

Buttercream Decorating Icing

SMALL BATCH

NOTE.—All ingredients should be at room temperature.

2   cups vegetable shortening (Crisco, Spry, etc.)
     or
½ cup butter and
1½ cups shortening

> *a*) Mix shortening, or shortening and butter, smooth on *slowest* speed of machine, or by hand. (At each stage, mix batch until it is smooth, but as little as possible.)

4   cups powdered sugar
    Salt to taste
4   tablespoons corn starch (more or less)—in hot weather only

> NOTE.—Measure powdered sugar before sifting it.

> *b*) Sift powdered sugar and salt (and corn starch, if weather is hot).
> *c*) Add *one-half* this sifted mixture to the shortening.
> *d*) Mix the batch smooth on the *slowest* speed—as little as possible.

1   medium egg white
    Vanilla or other flavoring to taste

> *e*) Add *unbeaten* egg white and flavoring and mix the batch smooth on the *slowest* speed—as little as possible.

234

f) Add the rest of the sifted powdered-sugar mixture, and mix the batch smooth on the slowest speed—again, as little as possible.

g) Put icing in a tightly sealed plastic, glass or metal container, and store in a cool place.

NOTE.—When stored at a reasonable temperature, 60–70 degrees F., icing will keep for several weeks. Do *not* place icing in a refrigerator except under unusual conditions.

h) When icing is to be used, work it smooth with a table knife or spatula before putting it into the decorating cone. When using tubes with very small openings, thin icing with a few drops of water.

i) If icing is too soft because of difference in materials or temperature, add *sifted* powdered sugar.

j) If icing is too stiff, add a little egg white or cold water.

LARGE BATCH

1   lb. butter

a) Take butter out of refrigerator an hour or two before using it, to allow it to come to room temperature.

NOTE.—If butter is used soon after it is removed from the refrigerator, cut it into small pieces and cream it alone in a small machine bowl until it becomes a soft paste.

2   lbs. 8 oz. shortening

b) Cream butter and shortening together on *slow* speed in a small machine bowl.

6   lbs. powdered sugar*
8   oz. corn starch*
½   oz. salt

NOTE.—During very hot weather, use 6½ lbs. powdered sugar and 12 oz. corn starch.

c) Sift dry ingredients together twice.

d) Stop machine, and scrape the mix down with a bowl knife.

e) Mix shortening blend smooth on slow speed again.

f) Then stop the machine and add *one-half* of the sifted dry ingredients.

g) Mix smooth on *slow* speed.

5 oz. egg whites
¾ oz. vanilla (variable)

h) Weigh egg whites and vanilla together.

i) Stop machine and add egg whites and vanilla to mix.

j) Mix smooth on *slow* speed.

k) Stop machine and scrape the mix down with a bowl knife.

l) Mix smooth again on *slow* speed.

m) Stop machine and add the rest of the sifted dry ingredients to mix (see f).

n) Mix smooth on *slow* speed.

o) Stop machine and scrape the mix down with a bowl knife.

p) Mix smooth once more, always on *slow* speed.

q) Stop machine.

r) Put unused icing in tightly covered can or jar. Store it in a cool place when it is not in use.

s) Always let icing come to room temperature before it is used.

Index